In the Public Interest

Protecting Whistleblowers and Those Who Speak Out

Peter Bowden

In the Public Interest: Protecting Whistleblowers and Those Who Speak Out
First edition, Second printing

Author
Peter Bowden

Cover designer
Christopher Besley, Besley Design.

ISBN: 978-0-7346-1186-4 (print)
ISBN: 978-0-7346-2066-8 (ePDF)

Published by:
Tilde Publishing and Distribution
PO Box 72
Prahran VIC 3181 Australia
www.tilde.com.au

Contents

About the author

Formerly Professor of Administrative Studies at the University of Manchester, and, immediately prior, Coordinator of the MBA Program at Monash University, Peter Bowden has worked with and consulted for the World Bank, the Asian Development Bank, and agencies of the United Nations. Since 2003, Peter has concentrated on teaching, writing and research in strengthening institutional ethical practices. Currently, he works through the Department of Philosophy at the University of Sydney in Australia.

His most recent book, *Applied Ethics,* drew on members and associates of the Australian Association for Professional and Applied Ethics. He has also published on strategic management practices in the public sector and in business.

Preface

This book is aimed at strengthening ethical practices in our institutions of government and in our business organisations. It does this through providing a background in whistleblowing practices that encourage people in organisations to expose wrongdoings that they encounter. It is almost axiomatic that those closest to the wrong would be first to notice. If they expose the wrongdoing, then the organisation – or society in general – can take action to correct it. The net effect is a stronger, more ethical society. The opening chapter outlines a long series of studies that demonstrate the effectiveness of blowing the whistle on wrongdoing. It is an effectiveness that covers many sectors of society.

But whistleblowers are crucified, or, to use the term in this book, are subject to retaliation. Governments, therefore, with increasing frequency, are introducing systems to protect them. But those who want to expose a wrongdoing in an organisation need to know how to protect themselves – not only by using the legal and administrative systems in their country of work, but also by knowing what they themselves can do personally. They also need to be informed of these possibilities in their training for work. Most of all, the many courses in ethics in our colleges and universities, or in the workplace itself, should provide students with this information. And a research base from which further improvements are possible should also be established.

The current systems work reasonably well, but they are not perfect. Most people cannot yet speak out freely against a wrongdoing that they encounter in their workplace without suffering some consequence. This book, therefore, is also aimed at those who can bring about the improvements that are needed – the legislators and administrators who devise and manage the systems, but also those researchers who are seeking new improvements or checking on the improvements that are being adopted. Hopefully, the same teachers that provide the courses will contribute to the research.

The recent revelations of Edward Snowden have raised the issue of what exactly *is* whistleblowing. Some claim he is a whistleblower, while others deny this vehemently. It is an area of contention that is treated, along with related national security issues, in the final chapter of the book. But so that at least the bulk of the book can treat the different issues in whistleblowing on a comparable basis, the different definitions are examined in Chapter 2.

The differences are not major. The more widely-accepted definition is, for the most part, adopted for this book – "the disclosure by organizational members ... of illegal, immoral or illegitimate practices under the control of their employers".[1]

---

[1] See Chapter 2 – What is whistleblowing?

Others connected with that organisation or institution – e.g. contractors, volunteers, and even associates – may also see wrongdoing and should also be able to speak out. And that speaking out, if soundly supported, should be investigated and the whistleblower should be protected. Additionally, that speaking out to the public at large could be through the media. These options have, thus, been included in a slightly wider definition.

The chapter does make clear, however, that social activism by one person mounting a campaign against an issue that they have encountered – occasionally described by the media as a 'whistleblower' – is not actually whistleblowing. Whistleblowing requires an organisational setting if the various protection and investigative measures are to operate.

Unfortunately, the world has not yet reached an agreement on what is a wrong. The various administrative and legal authorities have therefore provided lists of wrongs which they will investigate and for which they will provide protection to a whistleblower. An employee might *think* that he or she has witnessed a wrong, but if it is not covered by the legislation, then their complaint will have little impact.

Chapter 3 describes a number of these lists, most of which are short, containing not much more than half dozen items. They do vary within countries, and certainly among countries. The chapter concludes, therefore, with a plea to the authorities and the voluntary whistleblower support and research agencies to seek a common agreement on wrongs. If a common list were developed, the disclosure of which would attract protection and investigation, then the difficulties facing whistleblower would be considerably eased.

Chapter 3 also outlines some of the more common theories in moral philosophy on what are unethical actions – many of which are in disagreement. It is not certain, therefore, that, if you disclose an action you think is wrong, you will be protected.

The reader will also note that, interspersed throughout the chapters of this book, are a number of whistleblower stories. They range from a nurse in a small hospital in a Queensland rural town, to Deep Throat – the whistleblower who brought about the resignation of the President of the United States. Each of the stories illustrates one or more of the whistleblowing issues in this book. One such issue is the conflict between the individual whistleblower and the organisation. The individual believes that they are in the right. Those within the organisation may condemn them for the threat they bring to their organisation, to their jobs, or to their security. Chapter 4 explores the evolutionary theories behind this aspect of human behaviour. We, as members of the human race, have drives for good and for bad within us. One fosters cooperation, i.e. the ethical behaviour that supports the success of the group and those within it. The reverse drive is the attack on those who are seen to compete with or bring harm to the group. Chapter 4 provides a background to the evolutionary behaviours behind those who blow the whistle and those who retaliate against them. In essence, the chapter is saying that whistleblowing and the associated retribution are at the core of human behaviour.

The complexity behind these competing human behaviours is one of the signs that a complete answer to enabling people to speak out freely against wrongdoing will be a long time in the making. There are several other signs that developing a full whistleblower protection system will not be created readily. One is the ease with which the organisation can attack the whistleblower, and yet deny that it is a retaliatory act. Chapter 5 illustrates the many ways in which the organisation can retaliate. Despite the growth in whistleblower protection measures in recent years, several authors conclude that it will still be primarily up to the whistleblower to protect himself or herself. This chapter provides the methods suggested by the major whistleblower support groups, including Transparency International, in which whistleblowers can themselves strengthen that protection.

One of the more successful whistleblower laws has been the US *False Claims Act* (FCA), introduced by Abraham Lincoln at the time of the US Civil War to stop shoddy supply contractors fleecing the Union. It has been in continuous operation since, and has recently been extended to other legislation to prevent corporate meltdowns such as those of Enron, WorldCom, or Tyco, or a re-occurrence of the global financial crisis. That contractors would supply rotting foodstuffs or inoperable equipment to its own army is difficult to comprehend. Nevertheless, the need still exists for legislation that protects governments from illicit contracting. Modern FCA legislation in the US has extracted billions of dollars for false invoicing or false income reporting from some of the world's largest and best-known companies. In the US, the whistleblower is given a small share of these earnings; Australia and the UK do not have this legislation.

A recent inquiry in the UK, outlined in Chapter 6, rejected a False Claims Act for that country on the basis that it was inconsistent with the culture and philosophy of the UK, and that it undermined the moral stance of a genuine whistleblower. This conclusion is difficult to comprehend, since the net effect would be to stop a wrongdoing – e.g. to prevent business organisations from ripping off the public purse. At the same time, the US program frees up billions of dollars for spending on the social needs of that country.

Chapter 7 documents one of the more serious concerns encountered in whistleblowing systems worldwide – the failure of regulatory agencies to consistently follow up and action the information supplied to them by whistleblowers. This problem requires additional research, but a number of reasons are possible – from inadequate investigative resources, to the difficulties faced by a bureaucracy in investigating a wrongdoing. Chapter 7 also advises whistleblowers on the steps open to them to better ensure that regulators follow up and take action.

One of the initial objectives of this book was to strengthen the teaching of whistleblowing, particularly in ethics courses. Effective teaching requires students to be aware of the laws that protect them if they want to speak out against wrongdoing. Once in the workforce, they need to be able to access the laws and administrative support systems, and be aware of their limitations. It also requires that the whistleblower be able to protect himself or herself. The subsequent three chapters, Chapters 8, 9 and 10, outline the systems of the United States, the United Kingdom, and Australia. The first two, at least, help profile the variations that are currently operating in whistleblower protection systems around the world, the US being the more advanced. Australia provides an excellent example of a *second tier* country that provides the *appearance* of supporting those who wish to speak out, but not the substance. Canada, South Africa, and one or two of the European countries would also be in this second tier category. These chapters are intended to assist in teaching and guiding the whistleblower as he or she searches for whatever protection is offered in their country. These chapters also highlight weaknesses particular to each country.

Chapter 11 attempts to bring it all together. It is not the last chapter, however, for the reasons noted below. Chapter 11 endorses the guiding principles for whistleblower legislation put out by Transparency International, while also setting out recommendations for strengthening existing processes, many of which have been noted in the above paragraphs. These points would include providing a more formal imprimatur to the current voluntary national support agencies, or, alternatively, establishing a national office to support whistleblowers. One of the tasks of this agency in each country would also be to provide assistance in distinguishing those whistleblowers who are complaining for personal reasons, from those who are disclosing a wrong. The chapter also documents those areas where additional progress is needed. Among these tasks would be: seeking methods of strengthening the investigative process; developing a list of wrongs that can be agreed internationally; searching for the one whistleblower law to cover private enterprise as well as the public sector; and, finally, supporting the dissemination of information, including the teaching of whistleblower support practices.

The final chapter covers an issue that has only surfaced in the public conscience in recent years – that of blowing the whistle on wrongs committed in the name of national security. Edward Snowden is the prime example, but Bradley Manning, now Chelsea Manning, and Julian Assange are among those included. Informants of CIA torture practices are also an issue. It is a concern that may seem new, but that has possibly arisen many times in the past. One example is Georges Picquart, the French Army whistleblower responsible for exposing the truth in the Dreyfus Affair, who was himself cashiered from the army in 1898 and imprisoned for bringing the French Army into disrepute – and thus putting the French nation at risk. Picquart was eventually exonerated.

If this preface may anticipate the findings of that chapter, they are that, provided the whistleblower commits no wrong (which in most cases is to put lives at risk), then an open and democratic society must have that information. This chapter has deliberately been placed last, outside the main stream, for it will be many years before this issue is resolved. Hopefully, the many concerns with mainstream whistleblowing will be solved much earlier.

Chapter 1

Objectives
The 'why?' of this book

Introduction

This is a 'how-to-do-it' book. It has the simple objective of strengthening ethical practices across the institutions and organisations of our societies. It is intuitively obvious that people within or closely connected with an organisation will be the first to come across a wrongdoing within it. If they speak out, society has the potential to stop that wrong, or at least to prevent it happening again. As the research documented towards the conclusion of this chapter demonstrates, this 'blowing of the whistle' on wrongdoing has proven to be the most effective way of exposing unethical or illegal conduct by our business organisations and in our agencies of government. As such, it gives us the ability to create a more ethical society. It also provides an opportunity to bring about a fairer and more just society. For these reasons, whistleblowing practices and associated legislation has grown remarkably in recent years. For many reasons, however, this potential has not as yet been fully realised.

This book is aimed at furthering this potential – a potential for social and ethical strengthening offered to us by those who speak out in the public interest. It specifically targets a number of institutional groups who have the strongest potential to help build that more ethical society. The majority are individuals and institutions that have a multiplier impact – the ability to spread knowledge of whistleblowing practices.

The target audiences, those specific groups and societal institutions at which this book is aimed, include: teachers of ethics, researchers on ethical theory, whistleblowers, politicians and senior administrators, ethical practitioners, NGOs that work in whistleblower support, professional associations, and legal practitioners.

1.   Teachers of ethics in the many disciplines of our universities and colleges are a primary target audience, both in themselves and as vehicles through which students in their classes can be reached. Providing information on whistleblowing practices and whistleblower protections to students will enable those among them who come across wrongs in their working lives to speak out safely, or as safely as the current protections in their countries allow. But as will become obvious in later pages, many of the protections have not been fully perfected. Those concerned with teaching ethical practices need to contribute to the research on the many weaknesses that currently exist in the systems.

2.   The book particularly targets teachers and researchers on ethical theory and practice in philosophy departments throughout the world. Two reasons dominate. Firstly, whistleblowing is an ethical issue, for it is concerned with identifying and correcting wrongdoing. Ethics is a subset of philosophy. Courses on applied ethics exist in every philosophy department in the world. Yet speaking out against wrongdoing – its causes and its difficulties – is a topic largely ignored by philosophy departments and by moral philosophers who write the ethics literature. We believe that should be corrected.

     This second reason is more deeply philosophical. In this book we are treading near the edges of human reasoning. Numerous disciplines – philosophy among them – have told us that human beings are innately moral, and that our instincts for cooperation and even altruism grew out of our evolutionary past. Cooperation, support for and from the group that we belong to, strengthens the survival of the group. Another instinct – to defend our group against those who attack it – has the same origins. The reason why we so often crucify those who blow the whistle on us is because they have threatened our livelihood. The research that outlines this reasoning is set out in Chapter 4.

3.   Whistleblowers themselves still experience retaliation, sometimes very unpleasantly. This book aims to inform those who are thinking of blowing the whistle of ways in which they can effectively use the legislation that exists and that is supposed to protect them. The chapters on each of the countries covered by this book (the US, the UK and Australia) list and explain the current legislation. The chapters also point out where a whistleblower will not be covered, and where he or she has to be cautious. The protection is very different for all three countries. Nevertheless, even within these variations there are steps that a whistleblower can take to increase the chance of success, and to reduce the possibility of retaliation. *In the Public Interest* sets out those steps.

4.   Politicians and senior administrators are also a target. Cognisant of the benefits of exposing wrongdoing, as well as yielding to the pressures of those who want a more ethical social and work environment,

governments have sought to pass whistleblower protection laws. They have also established administrative mechanisms to operate this legislation. Some of it has been unbelievably complex. The most recent enactment in the United States, the *Dodd Frank Act*, for instance, is a document 2,000 pages in length. At times, an outsider gets the impression that politicians are not serious about stopping wrongdoing; that they are passing whistleblower protection laws because it is expected of them; and that they are also very aware that blowing the whistle, particularly on public sector wrongdoing, will rebound on them in a negative way. And so, they pass legislation that will only partially work, or that exempts politicians, or that starves the investigative machinery of skilled people or adequate resources. The following pages detail several examples of political recalcitrance.

5. Ethics practitioners – that is, people employed in our workplaces as ethics officers – are also included in those who can benefit from this book. The earlier Enron and WorldCom meltdowns and the subsequent global financial crisis have resulted in an increasing number of ethics programs being introduced into work places around the world. A formal and often mandatory whistleblowing system is probably the most significant of these developments, and the people who will be recruited to manage these systems will be critical in the future.

6. The NGOs – non-government organisations – that work in whistleblower support are another important target audience. And there are many around the world, and examples include Public Concern at Work, Project on Government Oversight, the Government Accountability Project, Federal Accountability Initiative for Reform, and Whistleblowers Australia. Most provide excellent support; a few are less than fully committed. We hope that some of the concepts in this book deepen their capability to learn from each other and to agitate more vigorously for more effective investigatory and administrative whistleblowing processes.

7. Professional societies, industry associations and trade unions create the codes of ethics that guide the actions of the members of their associations. They can also contribute in many more positive and direct ways. And, most of all, they can provide those members who may be thinking of blowing the whistle with the personal, administrative and even legal support to come through successfully and with minimum personal damage.

8. The legal profession is the final key target audience. And specifically, the lawyers who draft the legislation, those who enact it, and those who have to put it into practice are also targets. As will be seen, some of the legislation has proven to be less than fully effective. More importantly, perhaps, is the all-too-frequent occurrence when the legislation outstrips an organisation's or a society's ability to implement it. The legal components for reducing wrongdoing need to be soundly integrated

with the administrative abilities of the institutions and agencies of a country in order to effectively implement the objectives of the legislation.

This book examines three countries – the US, the UK and Australia. It is a coverage that provides a background on whistleblower management across much of the world. The three countries use different systems – systems that collectively will introduce the reader to the range of legislative and administrative options available to all interested countries. At times, additional information from other countries is introduced that helps realise the ethical potential of blowing the whistle, as well as the administrative and institutional difficulties that these countries face. Wide international lessons can be drawn from highlighting these difficulties. We, in the widest sense of this word, will all benefit from this book.[1]

Making whistleblowing more effective

Interposed throughout the book is a series of whistleblower vignettes. They tell the stories of whistleblowers, well known and unknown, from around the world. We have to thank Paul Stephenson in the UK and Toni Hoffman in Australia for some of the stories. Each of the stories has lessons, which hopefully are relatively obvious. These lessons build together, along with the research outlined in the several chapters, to produce the findings of this book.

It is not so simple, however, to outline the optimum approach for bringing about a more ethical society. Whistleblowing legislation has not resulted in stopping wrongdoing, or even, under some systems and practices, in significantly reducing it. A host of problems have intervened – including the situation where many will seen wrongdoing in their places of employment, but only a courageous few will report it. Most remain silent.

The research tells us that there are two predominant reasons for people not speaking out. One is fear of retribution – a fear that they will lose their jobs or be otherwise punished for speaking out. The second is a belief that nothing will be done anyway. As further sections verify, these beliefs are valid. This book, therefore, explores what the research can tell us so far about our attempts to solve these problems – but at the same time acknowledges that more work needs to be done.

The book draws on two sources. One source of information is a wide-ranging search and literature review. This search examined not only direct whistleblowing issues, but also reviewed the research that had been undertaken on the achievements and practices that have been adopted in the three countries and, on occasions, in other countries.

A second source is a decade of personal face-to-face experiences with whistleblowers, the problems that they face, and the efforts of many to bring about a resolution – both for the whistleblower and in seeking a more effective administrative program. These experiences have been interlaced with direct personal experiences in blowing the whistle and the retribution that follows it.

Some of these experiences are included in the whistleblower stories referred to above.

Current effectiveness in exposing wrongs

Extensive research verifies that blowing the whistle on wrongdoing by people in organisations is the principal method for exposing the wrong, and eventually for taking action to correct that wrong. This research is fully convincing. This section documents several such studies. They fall into two broad categories. The first category is fraud by employees against the company or public sector organisation – e.g. stealing from the organisation, or using its resources for personal use. The second type is wrongdoing by the organisation itself, where the wrongdoing is either committed by an individual, usually senior, or by a group of individuals. This wrongdoing is designed to benefit the organisation. Overbilling on procurement contracts in the private sector, for instance, or interference in public decisions for personal or political advantage in government are examples.

All research studies have confirmed that blowing the whistle on illegal or unethical action is the most effective way to expose it. Both types of whistleblowing are considered as effective counters. In the first category are studies by the Association Certified Fraud Examiners (ACFE) and by the large accounting companies. These studies found that employees were the principal method by which fraud was detected. KPMG[2], PricewaterhouseCoopers (PWC) and the ACFE[3] are the principal sources. PWC states that, according to the PWC Global Economic Crime Survey, for the public sector 31 percent of fraud is detected by internal tip-offs, 14 percent by external tip-offs, and 14 percent by accident. The report states that only five percent was detected by formal internal whistleblowing systems. We take tip-offs to be an informal blowing of the whistle, in the sense that the organisation does not have an officer appointed to whom a whistleblower would go.[4]

The ACFE 2010 report, its first world-wide assessment, reached the same conclusion as its earlier US studies based on information supplied by US companies – that the most common source for information on wrongdoing in companies worldwide was supplied by employees.

One study by the Universities of Michigan and Toronto also found that heading the list of fraud detectors were employees.[5] Probably the largest study was an Australian public sector survey that sent out 23,177 questionnaires to public servants in 118 agencies.[6] Those holding ethics-related positions in the various public services also found that employee whistleblowing was the most effective method of exposing wrongdoing.

The documentation of the research on speaking out is extensive and convincing. The benefits from encouraging whistleblowing are such that governments worldwide are strengthening their whistleblowing support systems. These developments are documented below. However, there are many issues still to be resolved – problems that are also described below.

The path is not a simple one

It should be obvious, even by this stage, that blowing the whistle on wrongdoing and protecting the whistleblower in the process is not easy.

This book is only one step in a very long journey. In one sense, it represents just one of the millions of small steps in the development of our current social structures. There is still a long way to go. In the words of AJ Brown, a leading whistleblower researcher, in a discussion on Wikileaks: 'the ultimate form of whistleblowing is progressing down a long and very unfinished road'. [7]

It is this road that has opened the newest set of deliberations on whistleblowing – that of blowing the whistle on wrongdoing in our national security agencies – an area of investigation barely visible when this book was first conceived. But it is not only this aspect of stopping wrongdoing that is unfinished. The problem of bringing about a society where any citizen can speak out successfully against wrongdoing is itself a long road. Perhaps this journey is best summed up in the words of Fred Alford, Professor of Political Philosophy at the University of Maryland: 'The whistleblower is the last man, not just tortured, but exposed and sacrificed so that others may see what it costs to be an individual in this benighted world.'[8]

Alford was writing in the context of Winston Smith, the 'last man' in George Orwell's *Nineteen Eighty Four*. It is hoped that this book is not about the last man. Rather, that it is a contribution to an ongoing and international effort to strengthen the ability of ordinary people to speak out against the wrongdoing that they encounter in their working lives, and to be successful in stopping those wrongs.

[1] The tern 'we' has been used at times throughout the book, not to signify a number of authors, but as a collective word for society at large.

[2] KPMG 2006, *Fraud survey 2006*, KPMG Australia, viewed 4 November 2013, www.kpmg.com.au/Portals/0/FraudSurvey percent2006 percent20WP(web).pdf.

[3] Association of Certified Fraud Examiners n.d., *Report to the Nations, 2006 – 2012: Key findings and highlights*, ACFE, viewed 30 March 2013, www.acfe.com/rttn.aspx.

[4] PricewaterhouseCoopers 2011, *Fighting fraud in the public sector*, viewed 25 November 2013, p.13, www.pwc.com.au/industry/government/assets/Fighting-Fraud-Jun11.pdf.

[5] Dyck, A, Morse, M, & Zingales, L 2007, Who blows the whistle on corporate fraud?, National Bureau of Economic Research, Cambridge MA, viewed 20 July 2013, www.nber.org/papers/w12882.

[6] Brown, AJ (ed.) 2008, *Whistleblowing in the Australian public sector. Enhancing the theory and practice of internal witness management in public sector organisations*, ANU E Press, Canberra.

[7] Brown AJ 2011, ' Weeding out WikiLeaks (and why it won't work): legislative recognition of public whistleblowing in Australia', *Global Media Journal*, vol. 5, p.5.

[8] Alford, C 2002, *Whistleblowers: broken lives and organizational power*, Cornell University Press, New York.

Box 1: My Story

Toni Hoffman, Whistleblower

My name is Toni Hoffman and I am the Nurse Unit Manager of the Intensive Care Unit at Bundaberg Base Hospital in Queensland. I came here in 2000 after several years of working overseas in Saudi Arabia and on the Sunshine Coast in Queensland. In 2003, a doctor named Jayant Patel took a position at Bundaberg Base Hospital as a surgeon recruited from the United States under the area of need visa status. He was soon appointed to the Director of Surgery position. Very soon after he started, we began to see a lot of patients with severe complications in the Intensive Care Unit (ICU). Complications that were normally rare became commonplace, and this was accompanied by other worrying trends.

Dr Patel would describe seriously ill patients as stable; he would refuse to transfer his patients to Brisbane – which was the norm for our small Intensive Care Unit. I first raised my concerns with the Director of Medical Services and the Director of Nursing six weeks after Dr Patel started. They were dismissed. I continued to raise concerns about individual patients and about the conduct of Dr Patel for the next two years. The Executive at the hospital continued to dismiss my concerns and attempted to discredit me. I was accused of having poor communication skills by my Director of Nursing, and given a book to read on 'How to Deal with Difficult People'. In the meantime, there were increasing lists of patients who either died or suffered severe complications. After a particularly bad incident in which a patient died because Dr Patel interfered in his transfer to Brisbane, I lodged a formal complaint with the District Manager and the Director of Nursing. Still, this was treated with disbelief and, although an investigation was requested, it was delayed for many months. After this major complaint was lodged, Dr Patel was awarded Employee of the Month. It had become apparent to me that all internal forms of complaint were going to be dismissed. There continued to be poor patient outcomes, and so I decided to take my concerns to the local Member of Parliament. I also discuss them with a reputable journalist who had been working on issues within Queensland Health.

My letter of complaint that had been lodged nearly six months earlier was read out in Parliament. Initially I denied knowledge of how this letter was leaked. At this time, the nursing staff in the ICU was threatened with gaol and dismissal for their actions. The *Courier Mail* journalist Hedley Thomas was covering the unfolding events, and when one of the nurses said: 'You know, there must be a trail somewhere, he hasn't become a bad surgeon overnight', Hedley googled Patel and found a history of negligence and malpractice dating back to 1981. In fact, Patel had voluntarily relinquished his licence to practice in the US for 'gross and repeated acts of negligence'.

It was then that there was public outrage. Patients came forward to tell their horror stories, Patel left the country, but was extradited several years later and stood trail for three cases of manslaughter and grievous bodily harm. In his first trial he was convicted on all counts, but in his High Court appeal this was overturned.

Although I was vindicated in the Royal Commissions and other enquiries, the personal cost to me for the past ten years has been extensive. I was awarded Australian of the Year Local Hero in 2006 for my actions in trying to protect my patients, as well as a Member of the Order of Australia for my services to nursing. I am very proud of these two honours, but I hope that organisations learn from this experience and do not allow this to happen to any more patients or staff. Dr Patel operated on some 1,400 patients during his two years at Bundaberg Base Hospital, and some 1,200 patients had to have some form of follow-up care from other doctors.

Patel had been fined by New York health officials and, in 2001, had his license revoked. In Queensland, he pleaded not guilty in 2010 in the Supreme Court to the unlawful killing of three patients and grievous bodily harm to a fourth. He was found guilty and sentenced to seven years, but appealed. These charges were later dropped in exchange for his guilty plea in relation dishonestly gaining registration and employment in Queensland. Patel, sentenced to two years for those charges, suspended due to the time already spent in prison, returned to the US in 2013 immediately after the court hearing.[1] A major benefit from the Patel case is that he will not be able to practice again. A second benefit is that registration responsibilities by State medical boards were transferred to The Australian Medical Board, supported by a newly-formed Australian Health Practitioner Regulation Agency.

Contributed by: Toni Hoffman.

---

[1] Calligeros Marissa. *Jayant Patel finally leaves Queensland,* Brisbane Times November 22, 2013. www.brisbanetimes.com.au. Accessed December 1, 2013.

Chapter 2

What is whistleblowing?

Probably the most extensively adopted definition of whistleblowing is that of Near and Miceli in 1985.[1] Whistleblowing is 'the disclosure by organizational members (former or current) of illegal, immoral or illegitimate practices under the control of their employers, to persons or organizations that may be able to effect action'.

Miceli, Near and Dworkin's study in 2008 endorses this definition, noting that it 'appears to be the most widely used'.[2]

It is an acceptable definition, capturing the essence of whistleblowing. The definition, however, raises some of the issues examined later in this book. It assumes that the report is made 'to persons or organizations that may be able to effect action'. This requirement raises the issue of whether such an exposure is sufficient. Many whistleblowers have successfully revealed information to the media. Box 5: Deep Throat, following Chapter 5, provides one of several such examples.

Exposure through the media does raise further concerns. Such disclosures are not always protected in Australia, the US and the UK, for instance, or they suffer from limitations being placed on them. Only one Australian state protects the whistleblower when he/she exposes a wrongdoing via the media. Even then it is a conditional protection, as will be discussed later in the chapter on that particular country (Chapters 7 to 9).

A second definitional concern is the 'under the control of their employers'. Not all wrongdoing is under the control of an employer. Richardson and McGlynn document their research into whistleblowing within college sports, where the wrongdoers are not necessarily employers. Those on whom the whistle is blown range from individual players and coaches to university sporting bodies. Those blowing the whistle are not employees, but fans, observers or other players.[3] The retaliation came from a number of constituents, in several different ways. Included were angry responses from fans who identified with individual teams and who were incensed at complaints levelled against a favoured coach or player. Neither the complainants nor these fans are employed by the university. In the longer run, however, fan retaliation can ultimately stifle dissent.

Another example of whistleblowing where the whistleblower is not an employee is Sheena McMahon, who blew the whistle on her estranged husband Noel, a detective sergeant who was using his badge to gain personal benefits through a range of malpractices.[4] Sheena was clearly not an employee.

Suppliers or contractors can also observe wrongdoing that needs to be investigated and stopped. For these reasons, this author has built on a slightly different definition in another work on ethical practices:[5]

> *Whistleblowing is the exposure, by people within or connected with an organisation, of significant information on corruption and wrongdoing that is against the public interest, and that otherwise would not be available.*

This definition requires the whistleblower to 'expose' the wrongdoing, in the anticipation that exposure to authorities who are able to take corrective action, or to the media, will facilitate that wrongdoing being stopped. Exposure to the community at large, via the media or other news outlets, can have the effect of causing the authorities to take action, or of causing the perpetrators to stop the activity voluntarily in order to prevent unwanted publicity.

That the exposure is 'in the public interest' is a key aspect of this definition. That is why it is the title of this book. Typically, public interest issues are actions that endanger public health, safety or the environment, or that raise anti-discrimination concerns or act in other ways against the public welfare.

> *An action that brings harm or has the potential to bring harm, directly or indirectly, to the public at large, now or in the future, is an action against the public interest.*

Chapter 3 on wrongdoing raises the question of when is a wrongdoing against the public interest. It also cites commercial whistleblowing services. These are agencies, often a branch of the forensic department of a large accounting company, although sometimes an independent company, who offer a service to employers to act as conduits for whistleblowers within the company. They offer a service by which the whistleblower can inform anonymously of fraud within the company (or government department). The question at large, therefore, is whether the exposure of wrongdoing that is at the expense of the organisation is in the public interest. Chapter 3 argues that it is.

A related question to this definition is whether the recent exposures of national security actions by people such as Julian Assange, Bradley Manning or Edward Snowden in the public interest. Are they then whistleblowing? Was Bradley

Manning a whistleblower? This question has generated strong differences of opinion, and it is covered in Chapter 12.

Definitions of whistleblowing

Jubb defines whistleblowing as non-obligatory:

> Whistleblowing is a deliberate non-obligatory act of disclosure, which gets onto public record and is made by a person who has or had privileged access to data or information of an organization, about non-trivial illegality or other wrongdoing whether actual, suspected or anticipated which implicates and is under the control of that organization, to an external entity having potential to rectify the wrongdoing.[6]

He also defines it as an act of dissent that is disloyal:

> A dissenting act of public accusation against an organisation which necessitates being disloyal to that organisation.

The version outlined in these pages agrees with neither of the above statements. Whistleblowing is obligatory rather than the opposite, and it is also unalloyed loyalty. The reason is simple. Our obligation to reveal an unethical action, and to work towards stopping it, cannot be seen in any other way than as an ethical demand on us. If we are to assess by the extent of the ethics of the action, then we must rank loyalty to the wider community or to the ethical precepts of society, at a higher level than loyalty to an employer. The whistleblower is making a judgement of the harm he or she may be inflicting on the organisation by exposing a wrong, balanced against the alternative of keeping quiet. It is a decision on which of the two is the preferred ethical action, a judgement that all of us make at some stage.[7] Our loyalty to society and to the well-being of our community demands that we act ethically and with justice. This demand outweighs any commitment that we may have to the organisation that employs us.

Social activism is not whistleblowing

What is also not whistleblowing is activism, people who at times speak out against an issue that needs correction. At times such speaking out is reported in the media as whistleblowing. An example is a Quaker-based website speaking out against racial profiling. Such profiling is the practice of law enforcement officers using a person's race or cultural background as the primary reason to suspect that the individual has broken the law. The website urges us to blow the whistle on police brutality.[8] Another example is an examination of sexual harassment against female university students in India, which is titled 'Blowing the Whistle'.[9] The article correctly rejects the harassment, but it does not describe an act or series of acts where a whistleblower identifies any particular persons who are subsequently investigated.

The pejorative terms

Terms such as 'snitching', 'ratting', 'flipping', 'informing', 'cooperating', 'whistle-blowing', 'turning in' or, in Australia, 'dobbing' have long been associated with whistleblowing.

The term 'whistleblowing', it would seem, is losing much of the opprobrium that it originally had. Part of the reason lies with the positive publicity attached to whistleblowers in the newspapers, as well as the accolades and awards given to whistleblowers. News media now cast, in the role of a local hero, any person who opens up wrongdoing to public scrutiny, regardless of whether it is the organisation with which they are associated. An Australian study demonstrates that whistleblowers are now highly appreciated.[10]

Australians overwhelmingly support protections for whistleblowers and their right to go to the media, according to a landmark poll. Debunking the notion that Australians dislike 'dobbers', the nationwide survey also adds impetus to calls for the Federal Government to introduce promised legislation to safeguard whistleblowers.

Sampling the views of 1,211 people, the survey found four out of five people surveyed endorsed the principle that people should be 'supported' in revealing inside information that exposed wrongdoing.

This more positive change was possibly signalled when Coleen Rowley (FBI), Cynthia Cooper (WorldCom) and Sherron Watkins (Enron) – all whistleblowers – were elected as Time magazine's Persons of the Year in 2002.

---

[1] Near, J, & Miceli, M 1985, 'Organisational dissidence. The case of whistle-blowing', *Journal of Business Ethics,* Volume 4, pp. 1-16.

[2] Miceli, M, Near, J & Dworkin, T 2008, *Whistle-blowing in organizations,* Routledge, New York.

[3] Richardson, B & McGlynn, J 2011, 'Rabid fans, death threats and dysfunctional stakeholders: the influence of organizational and industry contexts on whistle-blowing cases', *Management Communication Quarterly,* 1 February, Volume 25, pp. 121-150.

[4] Clifford, M 2013, 'The lone voice of the whistleblower', *The Irish Examiner* [Online], 05 October, viewed 30 October, 2013, www.irishexaminer.com/opinion/columnists/michael-clifford/the-lone-voice-of-the-whistleblower-245305.

[5] Bowden, P, ed. 2012, *Applied ethics,* Tilde University Press, Melbourne.

[6] Jubb, P 1999, 'Whistleblowing: A restrictive definition and interpretation', *Journal of Business Ethics,* 21(1), pp. 77-94.

[7] Bowden, P 2012, 'Harm to others', in M Schwartz & H Harris (eds), *Applied ethics: Remembering Patrick Primeaux,* Emerald Group Publishing Limited, Bingley. UK .

[8] American Friends Service Committee 2012, *Blow the whistle on police brutality*, 13 September, viewed 20 July 2013, https://afsc.org/event/blow-whistle-police-brutality-0.

[9] Bipasha, S 2013, 'Blowing the whistle: sexual harassment and redressal among female university students in India', *Learning Community – An International Journal of Educational and Social Development,* 4(1), pp. 13-17.

[10] Allard, T 2012, 'Support grows for corruption informants', *The Sydney Morning Herald*, 6 June.

Box 2: A Change of Career

Peter Bowden, Whistleblower

Many years spent in one type of work would suggest that most of us would work out our remaining years in the same sort of work. But, for this writer, this story says no.

Those preceding years were spent in Third World development consulting and advising the international development agencies, including the World Bank, the Asian Development Bank, the UN Development Programme and the Australian aid agency AusAID, as well as being on the management board of an Australian-based non-government organisation (NGO). It was a whistleblowing incident with that NGO on a project in East Timor that lead to my career change.

The UN-supervised referendum in Timor in August 1999 resulted in a vote for independence from Indonesia. It was met with destructive violence by East Timorese paramilitary groups with the support of the Indonesian military. The destruction, massive and widespread, frequently targeted schools. An international military force finally stopped the destruction and established a UN Transitional Administration. Many countries, including Australia, contributed to the reconstruction.

AusAID had contracted the Illawarra Technology Corporation (ITC) to design and manage many of their reconstruction projects. One of these was the provision of about $400,000 of school equipment and the training of students in East Timor. The Australian NGO won this contract in July 2000.

The procurement of the equipment was undertaken in conjunction with Timor Aid (TA), a Timor-based NGO which itself had been donated considerable school equipment from around the world. Quoting from the September 2001 KPMG review of the procurement requested by AusAID, the Australian NGO 'and/or Timor Aid initially attempted to earn significant profits by hiring equipment to the project (from TA stocks), when identical items could have been purchased at a lower price'.

The only procurement option (quoted to ITC) was hiring from Timor Aid for the majority of items. The 2001 KPMG report noted that the Australian NGO consistently argued that the time constraints prevented any other option. When AusAID insisted on purchase, although the cost of freight by air was 'excessive', 'The drop in price from TA hire to purchase ranged from 16% to 75%.'

In the end, all equipment was purchased, and ultimately left with the East Timor schools. I had contributed to the project from its earliest days, and again and again I had tried to push the Operations Director of the NGO for purchase, but without success. Board support was split, although I survived a specially-called Board meeting to dismiss me. I was asked not to attend that meeting. The reaction was sufficiently negative from the Operations Director of the NGO, as well as from some Board members, for me to resign from the Board in October 2000 and from the NGO early the following year. The blowing of the whistle, consisting of a phone call to the East Timor unit in AusAID, took place in November. It was followed up shortly after with a more formal letter. That letter specified the NGO staff behind the procurement. The KPMG inquiry was the result.

The experience raised many unanswered questions. A personal decision, taken then, to seek answers started with a search to identify the discipline that researched ethical issues. The result was an unpaid research appointment to the Department of Philosophy at the University of Sydney, a paid appointment teaching ethics in the Faculty of Engineering, and, a decade later, this book. Many, but not all, questions have since been answered.

The lessons verified since are that: (i) good people do indeed try to cover up wrongdoing; (ii) for some of us, to stop a wrong has a greater insistence than for others; and (iii) a negative reaction to the blowing of a whistle by fellow workers is near standard.

The still unanswered question for all these lessons is 'why'.

The difficulty when working with an NGO is that, by and large, these organisations do an enormous amount of good. The whistleblower is faced with divided loyalties, and the recognition that any damage to the organisation may impact unfavourably on the people it is trying to help. For this reason, other well-intentioned members of the Board did not approve of my actions.

Source: Peter Bowden.

Chapter 3

What is wrongdoing?

This chapter examines the problem of defining wrongdoing in a whistleblowing context. It does not examine all wrongs, confining itself only to those which a person in an institutional or workplace environment may encounter. They are problems which that person, if he or she exposed them, could reasonably expect the employer, or those in authority in that environment, to take action to correct.

As will be seen, however, there is little difference between general wrongdoings and those that may be encountered in the workplace. Wrongs such as racist attacks, stealing, verbal abuse, physical threats, lying, etc. – whether they occur within an institution or are encountered in the outside world – are still unacceptable.

Unfortunately, there is no universally accepted definition of a wrongdoing. The various ethical theories developed by moral philosophers over the centuries at times conflict, one with the other, and therefore do not provide a solid or useful basis on which to make a decision.

Another possible definition of wrongdoing is actions against the public interest, but even this generalisation does not cover all wrongs. Both issues are discussed further below.

The various national and provincial entities which have enacted whistleblowing legislation have, therefore, independently defined those actions which they consider wrong. These are the actions on which they provide protection to the whistleblower who reports them. The various legislative acts contain lists of wrongdoings which are then used by the regulatory authorities to decide whether a whistleblower's complaint sets out a wrong that will qualify for protection. If they agree that the whistleblower is disclosing an accepted wrong and the whistleblower has provided sufficient convincing evidence, the complaint will be investigated.

These lists of wrongdoings are developed by each national and provincial legislature as a separate exercise. There is a great deal of commonality among the various lists. Most, for instance, support blowing the whistle on activities that are clearly illegal, or that damage individual or community health and safety, or that affect the environment. However, there are sufficient differences between and among the various lists to draw the conclusion that a considerable amount of further cooperative research is necessary to establish what a government should consider as a wrong, and against which it will protect a whistleblower.

The legislative lists

The greater part of this chapter sets out and assesses a number of the lists of wrongs contained in the various research documents and legislative acts.

Exhibit 3.1 sets out a list of 38 wrongs which were identified in an Australian research project on whistleblowing. The project sent out questionnaires to 8,800 public servants across 118 Federal, state and local government agencies asking them whether they had encountered a wrong on the list. In concept, this questionnaire could be considered a near complete list of possible wrongs against which a whistleblower could lodge a complaint.[1] This detailed list of wrongs from the 'Whistle While You Work' research project covered a wide spectrum of wrongdoing types, grouped into seven categories. Whistleblowers drawn from the general workforces, as well as staff with core compliance duties, responded to these questions. The seven categories were:

- misconduct for material gain;
- conflict of interest;
- improper or unprofessional behaviour;
- defective administration;
- waste or mismanagement of resources;
- perverting justice or accountability; and
- individual or workplace grievances.

The study ran into some opposition on the basis that individual or workplace grievances were not wrongdoing – an issue further discussed below. Even when those grievances that could be considered personal and not in the public interest were dropped from the listing, the number of wrongs was in still in excess of 30.

A number of the categories, however, appear open to subjective interpretation, not readily open to legislative interpretation – viz., improper or unprofessional behaviour, defective administration, or mismanagement of resources. Negligent decision-making, misuse of confidential information, or waste of work funds are some other examples where a regulator might have difficulty in assessing whether a wrongdoing had occurred.

Exhibit 3.1

Wrongdoing

Misconduct for material gain

- Theft of money
- Theft of property
- Bribes
- Using official position for services/favours
- Giving unfair advantage to contractor, etc.
- Improper use of facilities for private purposes
- Rorting overtime/leave
- Making false/inflated claims for reimbursement

Conflict of interest

- Failing to declare financial interest
- Intervening in a decision on behalf of a friend or relative
- Improper involvement of a family business

Improper or unprofessional behaviour

- Downloading pornography on a work computer
- Being drunk/under the influence of illegal drugs at work
- Sexual assault
- Stalking (unwanted intrusion into personal life)
- Sexual harassment
- Racial discrimination against a member of the public
- Misuse of confidential information

Defective administration

- Incompetent or negligent decision-making
- Failure to correct serious mistakes
- Endangering public health or safety
- Producing or using unsafe products
- Acting against organisational policy, regulations or laws

Waste or mismanagement of resources

- Waste of work funds
- Inadequate record keeping
- Negligent purchases or leases

Perverting justice or accountability

- Covering-up poor performance

- Misleading or false reporting of agency activity
- Covering-up corruption
- Hindering an official investigation
- Unlawfully altering or destroying official records

Personnel and workplace grievances

- Racial discrimination against a staff member
- Allowing dangerous or harmful working conditions
- Unfair dismissal
- Failure to follow correct staff-selection procedures
- Favouritism in selection or promotion
- Bullying of staff

Reprisals against whistleblowers

- Other

Source: Brown, AJ (ed.) 2008, Whistleblowing in the Australian public sector. *Enhancing the theory and practice of internal witness management in public sector organisations, ANU E Press, Canberra, Table 3.5.*

Nevertheless, Exhibit 3.1 provides a baseline against which the following outlines of the wrongs set out in more important pieces of legislation may be judged.

The British *Public Interest Disclosures Act* (PIDA) 1998

The British Act has the major advantage that it applies to virtually all sectors and industries in the country, both public sector and private. As such, it (and for those countries that have copied it) is unique in the world. It is also much simpler than the requirements set out by many other countries. If assisting everyday members of organisations to identify and come forward with the ethical problems they encounter in their workplaces is one of the objectives of a whistleblowing system, then the UK system sets a high standard. As will be noted, however, PIDA and its administration does have some drawbacks,

The wrongdoings are listed in Section 43B, which specifies that whistleblowers gain protection when they reveal details of:

- a criminal offence;
- failing to comply with any legal obligation;
- a miscarriage of justice;
- when the health or safety of any individual is endangered;
- when the environment is likely to be damaged; and
- concealing any of the above matters.

One of these, a miscarriage of justice, is not fully clear. That term generally indicates a person wrongfully convicted, but the term is possibly wide enough to trigger a whistleblowing complaint. The issue with Section 43 B is whether it is wide enough. The UK government is currently inquiring into the adequacy of this Act, and has as one of its concerns the question of whether this list encompasses all possible organisational wrongs that a whistleblower could report.

The US *Whistleblower Protection Enhancement Act*

Enacted in November 2012, the US *Whistleblower Protection Enhancement Act* can be seen in contrast to PIDA. Section 743-3 provides for Federal employees to be protected from reprisal if they disclose misconduct that evidences:

- any violation of law, rule, regulation;
- mismanagement;
- a gross waste of funds;
- an abuse of authority; or
- a substantial and specific danger to public health or safety.

This Act captures issues such as mismanagement or a gross waste of funds, concerns that are also included in the longer Australian list in Exhibit 3.1, but not in PIDA. And the US Act does not cover environmental issues.

In the public sector, however, wrongs such as mismanagement, a gross waste of funds, or an abuse of authority are not easily defined in a legislative context sufficiently for a whistleblower to be certain of a wrongdoing.

The *False Claims Act* in the United States

Categories of wrongdoing are all connected with making a false claim on the US government. They include making the false claim directly by using false records as a basis for the claim, conspiring with others to make the claim, delivering less than the due amount of government money or property, and accepting a pledge of money or property from a government employee who is not authorised to make the commitment.

False claim cases are termed *qui tam* cases after the original Latin phrase describing this type of whistleblower action.

New South Wales *Public Interest Disclosures Act*

Interpretation of many of the above Acts may still be subjective. Even with the greater exactitude that is possible with listing the wrongs, it is still not possible to always be certain whether a particular action is in accord with the Act. The NSW Act provides an example. The interpretation of a wrong is frequently left to subjective interpretation by the regulator. This NSW Act is a 2011 modification of the original *Whistleblower Protection Act* 1994. It is described as:

> An Act to provide protection for public officials disclosing corrupt conduct, maladministration, waste, government information contravention and local government pecuniary interest contravention in the public sector; and for related purposes.

The various terms 'maladministration', 'waste', etc. are defined in the subsequent paragraphs of the Act. 'Corrupt conduct' has the meaning given to it by the *Independent Commission Against Corruption Act* 1988.

This last mentioned Act lists 25 categories of wrongdoing that describe corrupt conduct in Section 8. It is possibly as comprehensive a listing of wrongs as can be found in any legislation. Yet Section 9 of the *Independent Commission Against Corruption Act* modifies this listing, stating:

> *Despite section 8, conduct does not amount to corrupt conduct unless it could constitute or involve:*
>
> *(a) a criminal offence, or (b) a disciplinary offence, or (c) reasonable grounds for dismissing, dispensing with the services of or otherwise terminating the services of a public official, or (d) in the case of conduct of a Minister of the Crown or a member of a House of Parliament, a substantial breach of an applicable code of conduct.*

A criminal offence is clear. An interpretation of what could constitute a disciplinary offence, however, could vary widely. A potential whistleblower is a little more informed, for he/she knows that the wrongdoing has to be serious. But whether an act meets the legislated requirement is still a subjective judgement that the whistleblower or the agent undertaking the investigation has to make.

Equally unclear are the provisions on desirable ministerial conduct. A code of conduct does exist, but a public servant who experiences a ministerial directive that the officer considers wrong will not find much assistance in the code. An example would be the overturning of a professional decision made by the officer, to one which may better suit the political needs of the minister or of one of his/her supporters.

Transparency International

In its definition of whistleblowing, Transparency International lists the wrongs that qualify a whistleblower to obtain protection. This definition and the wrongs are:

> *Broad definition of whistleblowing – whistleblowing is the disclosure or reporting of wrongdoing, including but not limited to corruption; criminal offences; breaches of legal obligation; miscarriages of justice; specific dangers to public health, safety or the environment; abuse of authority; unauthorised use of public funds or property; gross waste or mismanagement; conflict of interest; and acts to cover up of any of these.*

It also includes perceived or potential wrongdoing such as fraudulent financial disclosures by government agencies/officials and publicly traded corporations, and finally human rights violations if warranted.[2]

This definition is wider than most other definitions.

US private sector legislation

The coverage of whistleblower protections in the private sector is by individual pieces of legislation. In all, there are some 57 Acts that protect whistleblowers, the earliest of which was the *Occupational Health and Safety Act* of 1970. This Act protected whistleblowers who disclosed safety and health violations. Since then, whistleblower protection has been developed for millions of private sector employees in a multitude of industrial sectors and occupations. Examples include asbestos in schools, consumer product safety, clean air, and banking.

The most recent legislation for the private sector is the *Dodd Frank Act*, which includes the incentive provisions of the *False Claims Act* (FCA). The reward systems of this latter Act have been included in the *Dodd Frank Act*; in the Internal Revenue Code (for blowing the whistle on income tax fraud); in the *Securities Exchange Act* (for exposing stock fraud and shareholder rip-offs – which include the *Foreign Corrupt Practices Act*); and in the *Commodities Exchange Act* (which covers commodity trading).

In summary, then, US private sector protection is massive. While the wrongs are precisely identified, they do create a whistleblower's nightmare, for the wrong that he/she may identify may not be in the industry or occupation in which the whistleblower works. Legal advice is invariably necessary, as the US system in the private sector leaves little interpretative freedom on whether a particular activity is ethically unacceptable or not.

Australian private sector legislation

Whistleblower protection in the private sector in this country is confined to the whistleblowing provisions of the *Corporations Act*. The Act is concerned with financial matters only, and in any case is difficult to interpret. It protects whistleblowers who report people who infringe provisions of the Act itself. Whistleblowers who reveal health and safety infringements or a range of other wrongs by the private sector have no protection.

Uncertain wrongdoings

Miceli, Near and Dworkin also note that acts such as firing employees arbitrarily, bullying or grossly misallocating resources, although not illegal, 'can be considered triggering events for whistleblowing'.[3] The issue at question, however, is whether they will trigger whistleblower protection. The US Merit Systems Protection Board (MSPB), in its 2011 survey of whistleblowing in the US Federal government, uses similar phrasing: 'throughout this report, a violation of any law, rule, or regulation, or gross mismanagement, a gross waste of funds, an abuse of authority, or a substantial and specific danger to public health or safety may be referred to as 'wrongdoing'. The data discussed in that report are from a survey of more than 13,000 Federal employees in 1992 and a survey of more than 40,000 Federal employees in 2010. The MSPB states that not all forms of wrongdoing are protected by law.

Table 3.1 indicates the percentages of wrongdoings from a 1992 survey and from the 2010 survey.[4]

Table 3.1 Wrongdoing surveys from 1992 and 2010

1992	2010	Wrongdoing
1.9%	1.8%	Stealing Federal funds
6.3%	3.1%	Stealing Federal property
0.2%	0.2%	Accepting bribes or kickbacks
5.0%	5.1%	Waste caused by ineligible receipt of funds, goods, services
17.9%	13.8%	Waste caused by unnecessary or deficient goods or services
11.9%	10.1%	Use of an official position for personal benefit
35.3%	38.9%	Waste caused by a badly managed program
3.9%	4.8%	Unfair advantage in selection of a contractor, consultant, vendor
4.8%	4.6%	Tolerating a specific danger to public health or safety
13.0%	17.6%	Other serious violation of law or regulation

The moral theories on wrongdoing

At times, a person will consider blowing the whistle based on their own subjective belief that a wrong had been committed. This may not always be the case. His or her first step should be to check the piece of legislation that they think applies to them. If that proves too difficult, and it will for most people on some of the legislation, then they should seek informed advice.

An allied section to this chapter, however, sets out the more significant of the moral theories (Exhibit 3.2). Most wrongdoing is intuitively obvious, although knowledge of the more significant theories may help in reaching the initial conclusion that a wrong has been committed.

There are perhaps 15 theories on what it is to be ethical (or unethical) that are outlined in one of Peter Singer's books on ethics.[5] They are frequently reduced to three: deontology, utilitarianism and virtue ethics, each of which has a number of subcategories. 'Internecine warfare' is the way one academic philosopher describes the conflict between utilitarianism and deontology (also referred to as Kantianism), at the same time promoting his theory of virtue.[6]

Moral philosophers who teach or write on ethics will support one or more of these theories. Peter Singer supports his own version of preference utilitarianism,[7] whereas Lawrence Hinman supports a multiplicity of theories. His wide-ranging text, now in its fifth edition, notes 'the diversity of ethical theories and the persistence of moral disagreements', and asserts that these disagreements are 'a sign of strength'.[8] Hinman does not cover whistleblowing practices.

Unfortunately for a whistleblower, the theories can create difficulty. The three theories will, on certain issues, give opposing answers. They are an inadequate basis upon which to decide whether an action is wrong, and therefore whether an observer should speak out against the action. They are the underlying theories for most courses on ethics, however, and may at times provide guidance for employees in the workplace. They are briefly outlined in Exhibit 3.2.

Exhibit 3.2

A brief survey of the principal moral theories

Utilitarianism

Utilitarianism is a theory which argues that the underlying morality of an action is dependent on its consequences – that we aim to maximise happiness, and minimise harm to others. The principal proponents of this theory are Jeremy Bentham, John Stuart Mill and Peter Singer. Although utilitarianism is possibly the most widely accepted of the moral theories, it is nevertheless strongly disputed by some moral philosophers.

Bentham defined it as 'the greatest happiness of the greatest number' (in 'A Fragment on Government').[9] This concept has been much criticised for overlooking the rights of minorities.

Mill argues that happiness flows from intellectual thought, and that minimizing harm is the overriding criterion: The moral rules which forbid mankind to hurt one another are more vital to human wellbeing than any maxims, however important.[10]

Singer asserts that we should acknowledge the preference of others.[11]

Deontology

A theory primarily relying on the German philosopher, Immanuel Kant. He has set out a categorical imperative which can be loosely described in two requirements:[12]

- act only according to the rule that you can accept as a universal law applicable to all; and

- never treat a person, whether yourself or any other, as a means to an end, but always as an end in themselves.

The term deontology comes from the Greek *deon*, or 'obligation, duty', and is therefore sometimes described as duty-based ethics. One of Kant's better known controversies, for instance, is that a shopkeeper should charge all customers the same fair price, neither dropping it to gain customers, nor raising it to gain income.

Virtue ethics

Virtue ethics is a theory which is based on the virtues. An action is morally acceptable if it is virtuous – usually defined as one of the many recorded virtues, or a decision taken by a person of virtuous character. The problem for this observer is that many of the virtues can provide conflicting answers. Justin Oakley and Dean describe virtue ethics in an organisational context as 'a plausible and distinctive alternative to utilitarian and Kantian approaches to understanding and evaluating professional roles'. They claim, in fact, the 'superiority of the virtue ethics approach to contemporary consequentialist and Kantian theories'.[13] It is also an advocate of this theory who describes the war between the theories as 'internecine'.[14]

Pluralist theories

There are several additional theories that attempt to combine the three main theories. For the most part they combine Kant and Mill. The more significant are those of Tom Beauchamp and James Childress, and Bernard Gert and William Frankena.[15] Gert lists ten rules, nine of which are harms that must be avoided while the tenth requires the observer to do their duty.

Many whistleblowing actions can be categorised according to one or more of the above theories, or indeed by the whistleblower's own moral code. Not everybody will agree that a particular action warrants blowing the whistle. A whistleblower may consider an action as wrong based on one of these theories. Sam Harris claims that 'there are right and wrong answers to moral questions', using science-based analytical thinking,[16] despite the fact that we widely believe that there are no ultimate answers on some disputed issues.[17] A whistleblower may believe that the action has caused harm, for instance, or simply that it is morally unacceptable. At this point in the development of moral theory, however, he or she will be protected only if the wrong is listed in the applicable legislation.

The public interest

Whistleblowing legislation is at times described as a 'Public Interest Disclosure Act'. This title raises the question of what is in the public interest. An earlier chapter has previously set out the definition that whistleblowing is the reporting of activities that are wrong or in other respects against the public interest.

The above paragraphs, however, raise the question of when an activity is against the public interest. The NSW Ombudsman in Australia, charged with oversighting the *Public Interest Disclosure Act*, states on its website: 'What is in the 'public interest' is incapable of precise definition as there is no single and immutable public interest.'[18]

The Ombudsman goes on to say:

> It would be true to say that what is in the public interest often depends on the particular circumstances, and each circumstance raises a range of considerations that at times conflict. Sometimes conflicting public interest considerations need to be balanced. Where such conflicts exist, it may be possible to address them through compromise or prioritisation. In other circumstances it may be necessary to choose one option at the expense of another. Sometimes it may be more appropriate to choose the 'least worst' option – the decision that causes the least harm rather than the most good.[19]

The issue comes up in a related but different context. Many companies and government departments have an internal whistleblowing system. The legislation at times requires such a system. Some companies will use a commercial whistleblowing service. These services are often a branch of the forensic department of large accounting firms, but sometimes they are independent companies that act as conduits for whistleblowers within the company. They will often offer their services on the basis that they prevent or reduce internal fraud. See Chapter 1 for the several studies which provide evidence that whistleblowing is the primary method by which this fraud is detected.

The question arises, then, whether reporting fraud against the company is in the public interest. Such fraud may be obviously against the public interest, such as stealing from the company or misusing company resources. Other wrongs, such as watching pornography on the company's computers in work time, are less clearly against the public interest.

This book takes the position that all commonly-accepted wrongs, when occurring within an organisational context, even though at the expense of the organisation, are against the public interest. The reasoning is straightforward. To condone a wrong is itself a wrong. Even though the public do not appear to be broadly affected, condoning a wrong is, in fact, against the public interest. A supporting reason is that a whistleblower who reports wrongdoing that is detrimental to the organisation, and not particularly against the general public, is sometimes treated adversely by fellow employees. The whistleblower should be protected against such retaliation. The study in Exhibit 3.1 documents retaliation experienced by whistleblowers when reporting theft against the organisation.

The overall lesson emerging is that the definition of wrongdoing is spelled out in the lists of wrongs contained in the various pieces of legislation and supporting regulations. For the most part, they are not in complete agreement. Further analyses, together with cooperative research from academia and whistleblowing support groups, will hopefully develop a listing of wrongs that can be universally applied – across all countries and for both the public and private sectors. Such an analysis will further assist potential whistleblowers in understanding what is a wrong, what he or she can report, and when then can expect protection.

[1] Brown, AJ (ed.) 2008, Whistleblowing in the Australian public sector. Enhancing the theory and practice of internal witness management in public sector organisations, ANU E Press, Canberra.

[2] Transparency International 2013, International principles for whistleblower legislation, Transparency International, Berlin, viewed 12 November 2013, www.transparency.org.

[3] Miceli, M, Near, J & Dworkin, T 2008, Whistle-blowing in organizations, Routledge, New York, p.5.

[4] Merit Systems Protection Board. Blowing the whistle, www.mspb.gov/index.htm.

[5] Singer, P (ed.) 1993, A Companion to Ethics, Blackwell Publishers, Oxford.

[6] Pence, G 1993, 'Virtue Theory', in P Singer (ed.), A Companion to Ethics, Blackwell Publishers, Oxford, p. 249.

[7] Singer, P 1993, Practical Ethics, 2nd edn, Cambridge University Press, New York.

[8] Hinman ,L 2012, Ethics, A pluralist approach to Moral Theory, 5th edn, Wadsworth/Thomson Learning, Belmont California, p. ix.

[9] Bentham, J 1776, *A Fragment on Government*, Cambridge University Press, Cambridge, 1998. Also available on line at www.efm.bris.ac.uk/het/bentham/government.htm.

[10] Mill, J 1861, *Utilitarianism*, Roger Crisp (ed.), Oxford University Press, Oxford, 1998. Also available on line at http://ebooks.adelaide.edu.au/

[11] Singer, P 1993, *Practical Ethics*, 2nd edn, Cambridge University Press, New York.

[12] For a more accurate version, see Kant, I 1785, *Groundwork of the Metaphysic of Morals*, Cambridge University Press, Cambridge, 1998. Also available on line at www.earlymoderntexts.com/kgw.html.

[13] Oakley, J & Cocking, D 2001, *Virtue ethics and professional roles*, Cambridge University Press, Cambridge, pp. 1, 3.

[14] Pence, Greg, 1993, 'Virtue Theory' in Peter Singer (ed.), *A Companion to Ethics,* Blackwell Publishers, Oxford, p. 249.

[15] For a description and discussion on these three theories see Breakey, H 2012, 'The Pluralistic Theories' , in P.Bowden (ed.), *Applied Ethics,* Tilde University Press, Melbourne.

[16] Harris S, (2010) *The Moral Landscape. How Science can determine human values*. Free Press, New York. p.28

[17] Harris , Op Cit p.29

[18] Ombudsman, New South Wales 2010 Public Interest, NSW Ombudsman, Sydney, viewed 22 October 2013, www.ombo.nsw.gov.au/__data/assets/pdf_file/0014/3713/FS_PSA_16_Public_interest.pdf.

[19] Ombudsman , NSW, Op, cit.

Box 3: The Pentagon Papers

Daniel Ellsberg, Whistleblower

Daniel Ellsberg, an analyst with the RAND Corporation, a US think tank, and a Vietnam veteran, generated a national controversy in 1971 when he released the top-secret study of US government decision-making on the Vietnam War. The releases were to the New York Times and the Washington Post. He was charged under the *Espionage Act*. He was also charged with theft and conspiracy for copying the then secret papers. The trial was dismissed in 1973 after evidence of government misconduct, including illegal wiretapping, was introduced in Court.

The decision to go public with the Pentagon Papers – which detailed deceptions regarding the Vietnam War spanning several presidential administrations – was a difficult one, according to Ellsberg. 'I decided it was worth a life in prison to do that,' he says[1].

A 1996 article in *The New York Times* said that the Pentagon Papers had demonstrated, among other things, that President Lyndon B Johnson systematically lied – not only to the public but also to Congress. The Pentagon Papers revealed that the US had secretly enlarged the scale of the Vietnam War with the bombings of nearby Cambodia and Laos and with coastal raids on North Vietnam. This information was not released to, nor reported in, the mainstream media.

The charges were later dropped after prosecutors investigating the Watergate Scandal discovered that the Nixon administration had ordered the unlawful wiretapping efforts to discredit Ellsberg. In June 2011, the Pentagon Papers were declassified and released publicly. Ellsberg is the author of *Secrets: A Memoir of Vietnam and the Pentagon Papers* (2002) and the subject of a movie 'The Most Dangerous Man in America: Daniel Ellsberg and the Pentagon Papers' (2009).

Ellsberg has come out strongly on behalf of Edward Snowden and Bradley Manning:[2]

> *Many people compare Edward Snowden to me unfavorably for leaving the country and seeking asylum, rather than facing trial as I did. I don't agree. The country I stayed in was a different America, a long time ago.*

Another view was expressed by President Richard Nixon:

> *[T]he sonofabitching thief is made a national hero and is going to get off on a mistrial, and the New York Times gets a Pulitzer Prize for stealing documents … What is the name of God have we come to? (Oval Office discussion, May 11, 1973).*[3]

Chapter 4

Why we blow the whistle
Yet crucify those who do

The answers to the question 'Why do we blow the whistle and yet crucify those who do?', as far as we are able to determine answers, might give us some insights into how we could encourage a more ethical society – by bringing into the open activities which are against the public interest. The second part of the question – 'Why do we crucify those who do?' – delves deep into human behaviour. It tells us that openly speaking out against wrongdoing will not be an easy development.

This chapter, in effect, briefly sets out the philosophical underpinnings to our commitment to cooperation and moral behaviour within our work and social groups, along with the reasons why we condemn those who expose any wrongdoing within these groups. Such an analysis suggests that speaking out against wrongdoing and the condemning of those who do are an intrinsic component of our behaviour. These factors, in combination with the complexities of the legislative and administrative systems that support and protect speaking out, suggest that developing fully effective whistleblower processes is not a simple task. It will be some while before we have optimised the most effective way to support those who wish to speak out against wrongdoing. As Kohn asserts: 'At some point there will be a change in the corporate culture … corporations, government agencies and most judges will acknowledge the benefits of strongly promoting employee disclosure of wrongdoing. We are not there yet – not even close.'[4]

The evolving nature of whistleblowing practices is a position reinforced in an Australian research paper: '… the present conflicted responses reinforce the need to maintain a clear, long-term vision about the role of public whistleblowing in integrity in government'. [5]

The first part of this question would appear to have three components to it. One is that we evolved with a drive to behave ethically, or at least we evolved as cooperative human beings, a fundamental aspect of which is that we need to manage our behaviour towards others in ways that encourage cooperation. The second component is the nurture side of this evolutionary argument – that we were raised – or at least most of us were raised – to observe basic moral obligations instilled in us as children. The third may be a by-product of the previous two. The research that tells us that we prefer to work in ethical organisations.

The second part to this examination is a search for an answer to the question that, if we have innate moral tendencies, reinforced by upbringing, why do we have a history of condemning those who try to stop wrongdoing, or of condemning those who speak out.

Why we are ethical

The literature on the evolution of morality is extensive and totally convincing. The following section gives a brief run down on the more significant research findings.

Perhaps the easiest way to get an overview of the research findings on the evolution of morality is to read the review by one author (Krebs)[6] on the work of Christopher Boehm.[7] Both are researchers on the evolution of morality. There is a remarkable degree of congruence and agreement between the two authors. The Krebs review is also available on line.[8] Boehm argues that the evolution of morality occurred in phases. The review notes that Boehm begins by identifying traits shared by chimpanzees, bonobos and humans (and going back further, by gorillas) under the assumption that these species probably inherited such shared traits from a common ancestor. He goes on to employ findings from archaeological research and from ethnographic accounts of contemporary hunters and gatherers to draw inferences about culturally-universal aspects of the social behaviour of early humans who lived in the late Pleistocene era, about 45,000 years ago. Then, moving to an explanatory level of analysis, Boehm uses evolutionary theory to develop 'working hypotheses' that account for the differences between archaic humans and humans who lived in the Pleistocene era.

Finally, Boehm notes differences between the social behaviours of modern humans and the social behaviours of hunters and gatherers, and offers a brief explanation for these differences.

It is important to note that Boehm is well qualified to accomplish these tasks, not only because of his theoretical background but also because of his hands-on experiences observing chimpanzees (early in his career, under the tutelage of Jane Goodall). It is the latter's observations on chimpanzee behaviour, however, that we note later as a contributing reason to why whistleblowers suffer retaliation.

One other aspect of the reviewer's version is the development of altruism and the place of the Golden Rule. Some authors may assert that whistleblowing is altruistic in origin, but such an assertion is doubtful. In the chapter on wrongdoing, and elsewhere throughout this book, it has been argued that whistleblowing is concerned with stopping wrongdoing. The version of the Golden Rule that might be more appropriate is the version espoused by some religions: Do not do unto others that which you would not want done to you.

A sample of the research that argues that we evolved with ethical propensities is listed and briefly explained in Exhibit 4.1. A significant percentage of these authors are philosophers drawing on the work of researchers in the evolutionary sciences, in anthropology, in mathematics and in game theory.

Exhibit 4.1

Writers, researchers on evolution and morality

Richard Joyce, a philosopher, reaches an ambivalent conclusion on whether morality is a product of our evolutionary history. He is less ambivalent that cooperation is acquired.[9]

Neil Levy, also a philosopher, reaches a straightforward conclusion that morality has evolved.[10] A review by Dennis Krebs, this time with James Climenhage, concludes:

> Overall, we recommend this book. Levy is a gifted writer and a clear thinker. He has taken the trouble to study evolutionary theory, and gets it right most of the time.[11]

Krebs also commends Levy's acknowledgement of cultural influences on the morality of our behaviours.

Matt Ridley is a scientist, journalist, popular author and a member of the House of Lords. One of the earlier writers on evolution and morality, Ridley traces the evolution of societal practices in ants, vampire bats, apes and dolphins, and finally among human beings.[12] He argues that the human race has evolved a capability instinct for social exchange that enables us to reap the benefits of cooperation. We ostracise those who break the contract. The subtitle of his book *Human Instincts and the Evolution of Cooperation* illustrate his emphasis on cooperation.

David Stamos is a philosopher of science. His work covers a wide range of issues on evolved behaviour – language, sex, feminism, race, etc.[13] He has a chapter on ethics and one on religion. He draws on Darwin extensively, noting that Darwin acknowledged the two sides of mankind. Stamos uses Wilson's term, moral ambivalence, arguing that reciprocal altruism is adaptive. He concludes that that it is not established that we have moral instincts, but we have a common core that is evolutionary.

Robert Winston is a medical doctor, scientist, television presenter and politician; and also Baron Winston.[14] His book, *Human Instinct*, has a subtitle 'How our Primitive Impulses Shape our Modern Lives', a suitable title for an examination of whistleblowing. Winston's book is primarily an examination of evolutionary theory. He supports Dawkins in the selfish gene theory, but also on the benefits of cooperation and altruism. He analyses various evolutionary theories – the prisoner's dilemma, game theory and tit-for-tat. He does not examine the full meaning of morality or that the ultimate moral objective is possibly measured by harm to others.

This brief run through of writers on the theories of evolution that impact on our behaviours is far from complete and does need to include two contributors – Franz de Waal, a primatologist and biologist, and EO Wilson, a biologist. De Waal, in a series of books and publicly available lectures, argue that the evolution of moral habits came from our primate ancestors. Wilson popularized the term 'sociobiology' in his 1975 book of that title, explaining the mechanics behind behaviours such as altruism, aggression and nurturing. The fundamental principle is that an organism's evolutionary success is measured by the extent to which its genes are represented in the next generation. One of his more controversial statements is that ethics needs to be removed from philosophers and placed in the hands of biologists. He argues against xenophobia. 'The treatment of nonconformists within the group grows harsher', a statement very *apropos* to the treatment of whistleblowers.[15] Written in 1975, Wilson's work attracted much criticism, particularly by Stephen Jay Gould and Richard Lewontin, both evolutionary biologists. Wilson's work, however, has subsequently gained wide acceptance and is now vindicated.

Even Darwin argued that our evolutionary history will have built into us a series of ethical values in that we are social animals, developing feelings of sympathy, obedience to a leader, faithfulness to the group, as well as defending and aiding other members – all of which he argues would support the group in its competition for food and even survival.[16]

Our final entry is Jared Diamond and the impact of religion. In his examination of prehistoric societies, Diamond also attributes our rules of social behaviour and, in particular behaviour towards those not of our group, to religious beliefs – beliefs which have been adopted by virtually all societies over time. He also argues that religion is a near universal need of the human race. It introduces a concept that is still evolutionary, but at the same time bringing in the values that we learned as children.[17]

Our nurtured instincts

Robin Dunbar, 'one of the most respected evolutionary psychologists in Britain',[18] examines the religious aspects of morality. A final chapter ascribes a moral objective to religion, along with several other purposes.[19] These purposes he places under several broad categories. One is providing coherence in an otherwise incoherent world, thus giving us a sense of greater control (through prayer and ritual). Another is to provide moral rules, and, finally, allowing a minority to exert political control over a community. A belief in an afterlife is evidenced by burials by the Cro-Magnon 25,000 years ago (although burial by Neanderthals up to 50,000 years ago are disputed). Religion requires second or third order intentionality, not developed in non-human animals. Dunbar states that religion's 'contribution to human wellbeing … raises … questions about whether the human race could do without it'.

He describes the slaughter of the Gombi tribe of chimpanzees as evidence of animal genocide – a story told more fully below in examining Jane Goodall's telling of that same story.

Our preference in employment and employers

It would also seem axiomatic that we would prefer to work within an ethical organisation. Such an organisation would tend to treat us fairly in a whole range of interactions between the organisation and ourselves, There are a number of studies that verify this assumption.

Possibly the most outstanding commentary on our reactions to our employers is Alberto Hirschman's 1970 classic *Exit Voice and Loyalty*.[20] Hirschman does not necessarily concentrate on moral issues within the organisation or institution with which we may associate. The subtitle of his book is 'Responses to Decline in Firms, Organizations and States'. He includes with morality other factors which would affect our reaction to the organisation, such as effectiveness, creativity and rationality.

Our response is one of three choices: exit, i.e. to leave; voice, i.e. to complain; or loyalty, i.e. to remain. Blowing the whistle, of course, is voice. Hirschman's opening sentence encapsulates his coverage:

> Under any economic, social, or political system, individuals, business firms, and organizations in general are subject to lapses from efficient, rational, law-abiding, virtuous, or otherwise functional behavior.

Miceli, Near and Dworkin[21] also note the disinclination of employees to work for a company that tolerates wrongdoing and squashes dissent, quoting in support Hirschman and the more recent work of Farrell and Rusbult.[22]

The other side of the story

Evolutionary theory has two sides. The other side is the question as to why we crucify whistleblowers. The answer is that we are two sided. Boehm's review endorses his 'characterization of humans as egoistic, nepotistic, and altruistic corresponds well to what we all experience in our everyday lives. People are not good or bad by nature; they are both'.[23]

We are not totally altruistic. Singer, in his examination of evolutionary theory and morality puts the case for both sides – that our evolved instincts bring both cooperation and selfishness.[24] A relatively recent article by John Armstrong argues that such behaviour is an eternal aspect of human nature, where, 'the tensions between our nobler ideals and the inner beast cannot be resolved'.[25]

The question as to why we crucify those who blow the whistle, and why we ignore or at times attempt at cover up wrongdoing by our organisation, has a particular niche in evolutionary theory. It is that we divide the world into 'us and them'.

David Sloan Wilson, an evolutionary biologist, presents the strongest case.[26] He argues that 'us/them thinking can be triggered very easily in normal people. The seeds of genocide are within all of us'.

Jane Goodall goes further. At the age of 26, she started working with the chimpanzees in the forests of Gombe on the shores of Lake Tanganyika, an observer of their ways of life. Now almost 80 years of age, she is still working with them. In one of the many books on her remarkable life, she writes: '… it is pointless to deny that we humans harbour innate aggressive and violent tendencies'; '…the dark and evil side of human nature was deeply rooted in our ancient past'. [27]

Goodall relates the story of seven of the 16 community males who withdrew from the central Kasakela area of the park to the southern part of their range, Kahama. Conflict between the Kasakela chimps and the splinter group erupted and escalated against Kahama. The Kasakela strategy was simple: hunt the enemy down one at a time, attack them brutally and leave them to die of their wounds. Within four years, the Kasakela chimpanzees eliminated all seven Kahama males and at least one of the females. The reason we can only speculate – the Kahama group were the 'out' group. The 'them' against 'us'.

Covering up

Retaliation, sometimes quite brutal, can be caused by a desire to defend a group from what is seen as an attack by a whistleblower. But it would seem that another response to exposure of wrongdoing is to hide the wrong from public view. That desire may arise from perhaps shame, or an unwillingness to be revealed in public as an organisation that has committed wrong. Perhaps the desire to hide comes from a belief that the organisation did no wrong, and in the broad scheme of affairs could do no wrong. That belief is held by individuals as well as by organisations. An example is the Catholic Church. *'Towards Healing'* was the Catholic Church's response in 1996 to the allegations of sexual abuse in the Church in Australia. Testimony was received at the current Royal Commission into Institutional Responses to Child Sexual Abuse that the program had issued $43m in compensation payments, at times requiring the signing of confidentiality agreements.[28] The surprisingly large payments made headlines around the country – a hush fund was one reaction.[29] There were many who had openly complained about church paedophilia – whistleblowers possibly. The response of the church was to cover up the wrongdoing, rather than retaliate.

[1] Ellsberg, D 2013, 'Snowden made the right call when he fled the US', Washington Post, 08 July, viewed 30 October, 2013, www.washingtonpost.com.

[2] Ibid, see also Ellsberg's appeals in the Private Manning Support Network www.bradleymanning.org

[3] Linder, D 2011, The Pentagon Papers (Daniel Ellsberg) Trial : An Account. University of Missouri-Kansas City (UMKC) School of Law, viewed 30 October 2013, http://law2.umkc.edu/faculty/projects/ftrials/ellsberg/ellsberghome.html

[4] Kohn, S 2011, *The whistleblowers handbook,* Lyons Press, Connecticut.

[5] Brown, A 2011, 'Flying Foxes, WikiLeaks and Freedom of Speech: Statutory Recognition of Public Whistleblowing in Australia', *Proceedings of International Whistleblowing Research Network Conference,* Middlesex University, London, 23-24 June 2011.

[6] Krebs, D. L 2011, The origins of morality: An evolutionary account, Oxford University Press, New York.

[7] Boehm, C 2010, Moral origins: The evolution of virtue, altruism, and shame, Basic Books, New York.

[8] Krebs, D & Denton, K 2013, review of Moral Origins: The Evolution of Virtue, Altruism, and Shame by C Boehm, Evolutionary Psychology, vol.11(1), pp.9-17, www.epjournal.net.

[9] Joyce, R 2006, The Evolution of Morality, MIT Press, Massachusetts.

[10] Levy, N 2004, *What Makes Us Moral. Crossing the Boundaries of Biology,* Oneworld Publications, Oxford.

[11] Krebs, D & Climenhage, L 2005, 'Book Review: The Nature and Nurture of Morality', *Evolutionary Psychology,* vol. 3, pp.133-141.

[12] Ridley, M 1997, *The Origins of Virtue, Human Instincts and the Evolution of Cooperation,* Viking Press, New York.

[13] Stamos, D 2008, *Evolution and the Big Questions*, Blackwell Publishing, Oxford.

[14] Winston, R 2002, *Human Instinct*, Bantam Press, London

[15] Wilson, E 1980, *Sociobiology. The abridged edition,* The Belknap Press of Harvard University Press, Cambridge, Massachusetts.

[16] Darwin, C 2003, *The descent of man, and selection in relation to sex,* Gibson Square Books, London, pp. 85,103, (originally printed 1871).

[17] Diamond, J 2012, *The world until yesterday. What we can learn from traditional societies,* Viking, New York.

[18] Brown, A 2003, 'Science to watch people by', *The Guardian,* 15 May, viewed 30 October 2013, www.theguardian.com.

[19] Dunbar, R 2004, *The Human Story,* Faber and Faber, London, p.168.

[20] Hirschman, A 1970, Exit, voice and loyalty: Responses to decline in firms, organizations and states, Harvard University Press, Cambridge, Massachusetts.

[21] Miceli, M, Near, J & Dworkin, T 2008, Whistle-blowing in organizations, Routledge, New York, p.34.

[22] Farrell, D, & Rusbult, C 1990, Exploring the exit, voice, loyalty, and neglect typology: The effects of job satisfaction, investment size, and quality of alternatives, Proceedings of the 1990 Conference of the Council on Employee Responsibilities and Rights, Council on Employee Responsibilities and Rights, Orlando, FL, pp.26-37.

[23] Krebs 2013, op cit, p.14.

[24] Singer, P 1999, A darwinian left: politics, evolution and cooperation, Weidenfield and Nicholson, London.

[25] Armstrong, J 2007, 'Taming of the Beast', *Sydney Morning Herald,* January 6, viewed 01 November 2013, www.smh.com.au.

[26] Wilson, D 2002, Darwin's cathedral, evolution, religion and the nature of society, University of Chicago Press, Chicago.

[27] Goodall, J (with Berman, P) 1999, Reason For Hope; A Spiritual Journey, Warner Books, New York.

[28] Armitage, C 2013, 'Royal Commission: 'No justice' in Towards Healing response', Sydney Morning Herald, December 10, viewed 10 December 2013, www.smh.com.au.

[29] Yeomans, J 2013, 'Hush Fund , Catholic Church paid $43 million to keep abuse secret', *The Daily Telegraph,* 10 December, viewed 10 December 2013, www.dailytelegraph.com.au.

Box 4: Whistleblowing in Japan

Michael Woodford, Whistleblower

In October 2011, British-born Michael Woodford was suddenly ousted as chief executive of international optical equipment manufacturer Olympus Corporation. He had been company president for six months; two weeks prior had been promoted to CEO. He then exposed 'one of the biggest and longest-running loss-hiding arrangements in Japanese corporate history', according to the Wall Street Journal.[1]

Mr Woodford has told how, at a board meeting at which he was not allowed to speak, he was ordered to vacate his Tokyo flat, return his laptops and telephones, and take the bus to the airport.[2]

Olympus originally claimed that, as its first non-Japanese chief executive, Mr Woodford had failed to understand the management style, but was later forced to admit that the payments which he questioned were part of a $1.7bn accounting fraud to hide losses on historic investments.

A report by a panel commissioned by Olympus accused the management of being 'rotten to the core'.

Woodford recognises that he was in a better position than many whistleblowers because he was in the most senior position at Olympus. He has stated that the fact that there were large amounts of money involved also helped, making the story newsworthy, and allowing him to get the focus of the world's media on the issue.

Whistleblower Michael Woodford has since settled with Olympus The chief executive brokered an out-of-court deal with the company over his sacking, believed to involve a multi-million dollar payout.

Woodford has maintained a vigorous media profile since then. He has made several claims that would interest readers, including calls for better protection for whistleblowers.

In his book *Exposure: Inside the Olympus Scandal,* Woodford revealed how the close relationship between Olympus and its audit firm KPMG over many years had reduced the likelihood of fraud coming come to light. He also attacked the decision of the Competition Commission not to seek automatic rotation of company auditors, saying a mandatory change is needed every ten years to prevent similar scandals at other companies.

Mr Woodford has also joined the Commission on Whistleblowing set up by Public Concern at Work, the British whistleblower support group. 'You may need legislation or a code of practice, requiring corporations to show they have whistleblowing lines,' he says. 'It would mean you could set up a whistleblowing line where it reports externally to a law firm or the best person internally, such as the chairman of the audit committee, or the chairman.'

An effective whistleblowing line should be separated from the executive of an organisation, says Woodford. What shaped his experience was the determination of the Olympus directors at first to deny the fraud existed before firing him and launching an aggressive public campaign to discredit him. 'You should filter out minor complaints, but if you have a serious issue where you think criminality may have been perpetrated, or an issue that is wholly against the public interest … and you feel uncomfortable raising it with your line report, then you should do this.'

Woodford dismisses the idea that many will not speak out against wrongdoing because of a 'climate of fear'. He describes it as 'a nice tidy expression', but adds: 'If you're working in a corporation, do you feel less fearful than you would have 20 years ago? Because of employment tribunals and because of the legislative framework … I don't think it's as bad compared to when I started working.'

Woodford says that the greatest hurdle for whistleblowers is often the fear of being victimised.[3] He also prefers the term 'bell ringer' to whistleblower.

Woodford is equally forthright on the issue of wilful ignorance at the top of organisations. 'You've got fiduciary duties to manage in a way that's protective of stakeholders' interests,' he says. 'I think moving from paying big fines to [making] officers liable to custodial sentences would be a good thing.' He recently urged companies to set up whistleblower hotlines.[4]

---

[1] "Olympus President: Will Do Utmost To Avoid Delisting" (subscription). The Wall Street Journal. Dow Jones. 7 November 2011.

[2] Much of this article was taken from The Guardian. Lawrie Holmes 29 October 2013 Auditors must rotate, urges Olympus whistleblower Michael Woodford, with the subtitle Former president criticises 'comfortable' relationships and calls for better protection for those who speak out. Also from The Telegraph article by Emma Rowley, 29 May 2012: Whistleblower Michael Woodford settles with Olympus and the many reviews of his book Exposure: Inside the Olympus scandal.

[3] Taken from an article by Woodford 'Why I prefer 'bell ringer' over whistleblower' Bells and whistles, Fraud magazine January/February 2013

[4] Newcombe, Tom. (21 November 2013), Olympus whistleblower urges companies to set up independent hotlines, HR Magazine on line http://www.hrmagazine.co.uk/ Accessed 22 November, 2013.

Chapter 5

Retaliation and protection

There is little doubt that whistleblowers suffer retaliation, sometimes quite severely. A classic description of the extent that they suffer retaliation is seen in the statement of C Fred Alford: 'They pay a terrible price.'[1]

POGO, the Project on Government Oversight, a US-based activist group concerned with ensuring honesty in government, make it quite clear in their report *The ART of Anonymous Activism:* 'The vast majority of whistleblowers suffer in obscurity, frustrated by burned career bridges, ... never achieving the validation or recognition they sought. Thus, for every success story, there are a hundred stories of professional martyrdom.'[2]

GAP, the Government Accountability Project, a whistleblower support group, quotes numerous examples of retaliation in a publication by its legal advisor, Tom Devine. Reprisal rates of 69 percent, 95 percent, or almost 100 percent (232 out of 233 cases) were quoted. Devine and his co-writer, Tarek Maassarani, conclude:

> *A public whistleblower should not expect justice ... The odds of a painful and protracted reprisal, on the other hand, are almost a sure bet.* [3]

Perhaps the most extreme retaliation against whistleblowers is found on the subcontinent. The Deccan Herald report, *Whistleblower hacked to death*, was about a Right to Information activist and corruption whistleblower who was killed in India. Three men attacked him with 'lethal weapons' in his village in front of his wife.[4]

India has a notorious track record with whistleblower protection, with many whistleblowers being killed. The Deccan Herald lists a half dozen in recent years.[5]

Many further examples can be quoted, including those that have been made into movies. Meryl Streep played Karen Silkwood in the movie *Silkwood* – a union organiser making components for nuclear reactor fuel rods at the Kerr-McGee plant in Oklahoma. She died on the way to a union meeting under mysterious circumstances. Silkwood had been investigating claims of corporate inaction on health issues. Jeffrey Wigand, Vice-President of Research and Development at Brown and Williamson Tobacco, blew the whistle on the effects of smoking. From Vice-President he became a school teacher (although he now runs a consultancy and speaking career on tobacco issues). He was played by Russell Crow in the movie *The Insider*.

The reasons for the retaliation are complex. An earlier chapter put forward the theory that the whistleblower is seen as attacking both us and our livelihoods. The retaliation against those who are attacking us is a defensive move, instilled into human behavioural patterns over several thousands of years. The references that assert this dual nature of the human race are convincing.

Organisational retaliation

The forms of retaliation are many and varied. Miceli and Near, drawing on a 1980 survey by the US Merit Systems Protection Board, identified nine:[6]

1.   poor performance appraisal;
2.   denial of promotion;
3.   denial of opportunity for training;
4.   assigned to less desirable or less important duties;
5.   transfer or reassignment to a different job with less desirable duties;
6.   reassignment to a different geographic location;
7.   suspension of job (presumably implying dismissal);
8.   grade level demotion; and
9.   other (specified by the respondent).

Most of these retaliation categories can also be found on the POGO – Project on Government Oversight – website.[7]

Rates of retaliation

The research on retaliation rates gives figures ranging from a high of about 90 percent down to 22 percent. This lower rate came from two recent and highly regarded research studies – one on whistleblowing in the Australian public sector,[8] and the second from the Ethics Resource Center (ERC) in the US.[9] The higher rates came from older studies. The Corporate Survival Guide, as noted above, documents very high rates of retaliation.

Miceli, Near and Dworkin, in an extensive survey of the research literature, tell us that 'estimates of the incidence of retaliation varied dramatically'. They quote research studies that range from 17 percent in 1980 to 37 percent in 2004.[10]

In short, there is a range of retaliation rates that have been measured. These rates seem to have dropped in recent years. There are two possible reasons that may have caused retaliation rates to fall:

- the word is getting out that whistleblowing can be effective and that policies and legislation are in place to protect the whistleblower; or

- whistleblowers are now heroes. The three female whistleblowers nominated as Persons of the Year on the cover of Time magazine in 2002 perhaps started this trend – Sherron Watkins of Enron, Coleen Rowley of the FBI, and Cynthia Cooper of WorldCom. The laudatory comments on Edward Snowden, who exposed the worldwide surveillance programs of the US the National Security Agency (albeit with equally condemnatory comments), continue this trend (see Chapter 12).

The growth in internal whistleblowing systems (managed internally or supplied by contract) has likely added to the widening of exposure to whistleblowing practices. Those companies offering an internal service, often by the forensic arms of big accounting companies, advertise and promote their service on the assertion that they reduce the cost of internal fraud. This growth is likely spurred by increasing legislative demands that companies install internal whistleblowing systems, as well as by the advertising and the research that document the benefits of internal whistleblowing systems.

Anonymous exposures

The nervousness and uncertainty that many whistleblowers experience, or alternatively the retaliation that they expect, cause many whistleblowers to make their exposures anonymously.

Anonymous whistleblowing has its drawbacks – the nature of the allegation will frequently identify the whistleblower. A second weakness is that the investigators must have sufficient detail to investigate the allegation in order to confirm its validity. Without the ability to interview the source of information, however, they may not be able to reach a conclusion on the allegation. They therefore drop the investigation.

Much of the current legislation requires that the whistleblower's identity be kept confidential in an attempt to minimise retaliation. Such a requirement is a worthwhile addition to whistleblower protection legislation. This writer's experience, however, is that keeping the whistleblower's name hidden is difficult and not always successful.

Some support NGOs assist the whistleblower in making the exposure anonymous. POGO, the Project on Government Oversight, is one. POGO claims that, by working anonymously, the whistleblower generally does not risk retaliation or jeopardizing his or her career. It is up to the whistleblower to provide POGO with the necessary information, documents or leads. This allows the whistleblower to expose the wrongdoing while lowering the risk of being attacked. In the past this process has worked with whistleblowers who remain anonymous even to POGO.

Protecting those who blow the whistle

Avoiding any retaliation is one of the objectives of whistleblowing legislation and its associated administrative machinery. In many countries 'whistleblower protection' was the name first given to the legislation, and it is still widely used. Such protection is, in any case, still one of the objectives of any legislation.

A limited number of mechanisms are available to protect whistleblowers from retaliation:

- Retaliation is forbidden by law, with fines or prison sentence levied for retaliation.
- The whistleblower's identity must be kept confidential, along with the information he/she supplied.
- In the UK, the whistleblower, if experiencing retaliation, can go to an Employment Tribunal and seek restitution for damages. In concept, the possibility of paying damages is seen as a deterrent to the offending organisation.
- The top-down imposition of non-retaliatory measures by senior management. One observation from the Australian study on public sector whistleblowing was that some agencies treated whistleblowers well, while others did not.[11] At that point in time, formal whistleblower support programs were quite rare, leading to the conclusion that the lower rates of retaliation could only be attributed to the ethical standards promulgated by senior management.
- Installation of a formal ethics program within the organisation, including the identification of staff to whom whistleblowers could report. In the ERC study noted above, 18 percent of employees said they did not report because they did not know whom to contact. Miceli, Near and Dworkin, in their exploration of approaches aimed at reducing retaliation, endorse the establishment of formal ethics programs, quoting other research programs in support.[12]

Protecting yourself as a whistleblower

A number of whistleblowing support sites contain advice lines aimed at helping the whistleblower stay safe. The Government Accountability Project (GAP) has produced a survival guide for corporate whistleblowers (see Exhibit 5.1). They, as shown by the suggested guidelines, are also aimed at helping the whistleblower be successful in achieving his or her objective of stopping the wrongdoing.

Exhibit 5.1

The Government Accountability Project guidelines

1. Consult your loved ones.

2. Test the waters of support among your workplace peers.

3. Before breaking ranks, consider working within the system.

4. Always be on guard not to embellish your findings.

5. Seek legal and other advice early.

6. Stay on the defensive with a well thought out plan.

7. Maintain good relations with administrative and support staff.

8. Network off the job; identify potential allies such as elected officials, journalists, or activists with a proven track record.

9. Keep an ongoing, detailed contemporaneous record as you go.

10. Secure all relevant records before drawing any suspicion to yourself.

11. Engage in whistleblowing initiatives in your own time and with your own resources, not your employer's.

12. Check for skeletons in your closet.

13. Do not reveal your cynicism when working with the authorities.

Source: Devine, T, & Maassarani, T 2011, The Corporate Whistleblower's Survival Guide, *Barrett-Koehler Publishers , San Francisco, p.47.*

Another list worth mentioning is that of Brian Martin in his *Whistleblowing: A Practical Guide.*[13] It does not draw on Australian legislation, but is aimed directly at whistleblowers and is for their own action. It is primarily a list of cautions – that is, of actions to avoid:

1. Trusting too much. Do not trust the company, your colleagues, or the investigator.

2. Not having enough evidence.

3. Using the wrong style. Shouting, hectoring and obvious disgust can be counterproductive.

4. Not waiting for the right opportunity. Do not speak out immediately, but wait until an opportunity opens up – a second incident possibly, or a confidential meeting with a senior colleague.

5. Not building support. Others are needed to support you.

6. Playing the opponent's game. They have all the resources, and you have very few. So do not compete through spending resources.

7.   Not knowing when to stop. Many whistleblowers are carried away excessively. It damages their case.

Our own list would endorse these recommendations. All those who work in whistleblowing issues are familiar with them, and particularly the last one mentioned – for example, the pages and pages of complaints or excessive emails that some whistleblowers send out.

The ten point process outlined below would place greater emphasis on using the legislation effectively, and on simplifying, even assisting, the regulator in making an initial assessment. Public sector whistleblowing, as outlined in subsequent chapters, faces hurdles in convincing authorities that it is a whistleblowing event that should trigger investigation and formal protection. It seems reasonable, therefore, to check, as a first priority, that the wrongdoing is covered by the legislation. This might at times be difficult, so seeking further information on the extent of the legislated coverage will at times require outside assistance. An effective whistleblower support agency should be able to provide that information.

It is useful, therefore, to lodge the whistleblowing accusation in a way that clearly states the wrongdoing and clearly states that your information warrants investigation. The evidence supporting the accusation should also be clear and, if possible, supported by colleagues.

The ten point process

Set out below are the steps that we believe will maximize the chances of success, and of survival, for the whistleblower:

1.   Find out if the legislation to protect whistleblowers covers you. Search for whistleblowing legislation in your country. Seek advice from your local whistleblower support group. In Australia, and several other countries, current legislation covers only employees in state government services. In the private sector in Australia, whistleblowing is protected only for offences against the *Corporations Act* or the *Workplace Relations Act*. These Acts are not effective.

2.   Read the Act that covers you. Particularly note those provisions that provide you with protection from retribution. Also note what you can reveal, and to whom it should be revealed. This varies from country to country. Finally, make sure that what you are considering revealing is sufficiently in the public interest and serious enough to warrant the difficulties that it will cause you, and the authorities who will investigate it.

3.   See if you can find others in your organisations who are willing to go along with you in support of your evidence.

4.   Talk your intentions over with your family and close friends. Their support will be needed. They may not be willing to support you.

5.   Gather as much evidence as you can of the dishonesty that you intend to reveal. Take notes; make photocopies. Remember that the person or organisation to whom you make the revelations, an Ombudsman's office or similar, will need to investigate your complaint. To convince them to take you seriously requires you to present them with reasonable and, as far as possible, independent evidence. Australian State Acts will protect you if you collect evidence that is internal to the organisation. Check if the applicable legislation protects you against the breaking of confidentiality clauses in employment agreements. The Ombudsman or similar will eventually need to convince a public prosecutor to prosecute and, with your help, to gather sound court-acceptable evidence.

6.   Go to a whistleblowers support group, your union, or another support body and talk your actions over with them. See if someone can find the time to come with you as a support person and a witness if you wish to make the complaint in person. Make sure they are convinced of your honesty and that you are not acting through disenchantment with the organisation or with your supervisor.

7.   For small cases, see if you can expose the wrongdoing without confrontation. Go to the highest person organisationally that you will feel comfortable with and whom you believe will work in the interests of the organisation. Some organisations appoint a whistleblower contact. For high level large scale illegal behaviour, go outside the organisation to an ombudsman or appropriate regulator. Ask that your name be kept confidential if you need to. Note that the legislation will not guarantee complete confidentiality for investigating the complaint. Your organisation may find out who made the accusation, but you can request confidentiality during the early stages of the investigation. Place the emphasis of your disclosures on the wrongdoing in the organisation, and not on any harassment or ill-treatment that you have received.

8.   Within your organisation, be prepared for personal rejection and retaliation. It will be very unusual if it does not come. Senior managers will resent the implication that they have been ineffective; some of them may even be involved in the wrongdoing. Colleagues will resent you as a threat to the security of the organisation in which you and they work. If the harassment continues, record details and threaten legal action. If necessary, sue. Most Acts give you the right to sue. Alternatively, seek a new job. Early consideration of this possible need will probably be in your best interests.

9.   The retaliation is often nasty, subtle, difficult to combat, and not always clearly tied to the whistleblowing. Keep notes on every act of harassment against you, even if it does not appear to be connected with your whistleblowing. As far as possible, be prepared for the harassment. It could come from an unexpected quarter.

10. If the harassment continues, see what other relief your legislation offers you (relocation, for instance). Complain to a higher level if possible, but

in the final analysis seek legal advice and take action for damages. If you complain about harassment, place your emphasis on the public interest disclosure; any harassment or ill will is a result of that disclosure. Also, follow up on the investigation of your complaint, as most jurisdictions are obliged to tell you what the outcome is.

And finally, if you do not win, if the wrongdoing is covered over without any action being taken, try not to allow any sense of injustice to dominate your life. Remember that you have had a personal moral victory in making the disclosure. Attempt, as far as is possible, to create for yourself a new life and a new job.

[1] Alford, C.F. 2002, *Whistleblowers: broken lives and organizational power,* Cornell University Press, New York.

[2] Project on Government Oversight 2010, *gp-Whistleblower Manual-Chapter-1*, POGO, viewed 30 August 2012, www.scribd.com/doc/38474290/gp-WhistleblowerManual-Chapter1, p.1.

[3] Devine, T, & Maassarani, T 2011, The Corporate Whistleblower's Survival Guide, Barrett-Koehler Publishers , San Francisco, p.43.

[4] 'Whistleblower Hacked to Death' 2012, Deccan Herald, 20 November, viewed 22 November 2013, www.deccanherald.com.

[5] "The New Mafia Raj , Deccan Herald, 4 December 2013, viewed 4 December, 2013 www.deccanherald.com.

[6] Miceli, M & Near, J 2002, 'What makes *whistle-blowers* effective?', *Human Relations*, vol. 55 (4), p. 472.The study tested four hypotheses on what made whistleblowing effective. Described as 'exploratory,'the study concluded with the statement: "Clearly, more research is needed" p.476.

[7] Project on Government Oversight 2010, *op. cit.*

[8] Brown, AJ (ed.) 2008, *Whistleblowing in the Australian public sector. Enhancing the theory and practice of internal witness management in public sector organisations,* ANU E Press, Canberra.

[9] Ethics Resource Centre National Business Ethics Survey 2005: How Employees View Ethics in Their Organizations 1994-2005.

[10] Miceli, M, Near, J & Dworkin, T 2008, *Whistle-blowing in organizations,* Routledge, New York. p.24.

[11] Brown, AJ 2008, *op. cit.*

[12] Miceli, M, Near,J,& Dworkin T 2008, *op. cit.*

[13] Martin, B 2013, *Whistleblowing: A Practical Guide,* Irene Publishing, Sparsnas, Sweden. This is a revised and updated version of his Whistleblower's Handbook: How to Be an Effective Resister (1999), Jon Carpenter, Charlbury, UK and Envirobook, Sydney.

Box 5: Deep Throat

Mark Felt, Whistleblower

Democracy Now, an activist website, cites Daniel Ellsberg as America's most famous whistleblower. The website may be right, but there are many contenders. One, Mark Felt, or 'Deep Throat', must be a major contender. His whistleblowing, after all, caused the resignation of a President of the United States.

Deep Throat is the pseudonym given to Felt, a Federal Bureau of Investigation Associate Director. Felt secretly provided Bob Woodward and Carl Bernstein of The Washington Post in 1972 with details on United States President Richard Nixon's involvement in the Watergate scandal. His identity remained a secret.

In 2005, thirty-one years after Nixon's resignation and eleven years after Nixon's death, Deep Throat was revealed to be Felt.

On 28 February 1973, Nixon and John Dean, a White House advisor, tagged Felt as the potential leaker. He was, Dean told Nixon, 'the only person that knows'. But Nixon was sceptical, believing that no one would risk their career to become an informant. According to a tape recording from that day, Nixon said:

> You know, suppose that Felt comes out and unwraps the whole thing? What does that do to him? He's in a very dangerous situation ... The informer is not wanted in our society. Either way, that's the one thing people do sort of line up against. They ... say, 'Well, that (expletive) informed, I don't want him around.'[1]

The Watergate scandal began with the arrests for breaking into the Democratic National Committee headquarters at the Watergate complex in Washington DC on 17 June 1972. The Federal Bureau of Investigation (FBI) connected the burglars to the Committee for the Re-Election of the President, the official organization of Nixon's campaign. In July 1973, in evidence to the Senate Watergate Committee, it was revealed that President Nixon had used a tape-recording system, which implicated the President in his attempts to cover up the break-in. The US Supreme Court unanimously ruled that the president had to hand over the tapes to government investigators.

Facing near certain impeachment in the House of Representatives and a possible conviction in the Senate, Nixon resigned the presidency on August 9, 1974. Gerald Ford, the incoming President, issued Nixon a pardon.

In 1973, Felt had been meeting secretly with Bob Woodward and Carl Bernstein of the Washington Post at 2am in a Washington garage. He supplied them with a series of sensational scoops about the abuse of presidential power. Internally, within the FBI, Felt denounced the Post stories as an amalgam of 'fiction and half-truths,' combined with some genuine information. To deflect attention from himself, he ordered an investigation into the latest leak. Woodward and Bernstein subsequently published a best seller, *All the President's Men* on the affair.

Felt is at times portrayed as having mixed motives[2] – one as a courageous whistleblower, personally obliged and driven to reveal information in the public interest. However, detractors depict him as driven by overreaching personal ambition. There is little doubt, however, that if he had revealed his identity, his career would have been finished. Felt died in 2008.

---

[1] Quote from Public Concern at Work "The Biennial Review 2005 "Where's the public interest?". Also Balz, D 2005, 'Source was conflicted on his role', *The Washington Post*, June 1, viewed 28 November 2013, http://www.washingtonpost.com

[2] Dobbs, M 2005,'Watergate and the two lives of Mark Felt: Roles as FBI official, 'Deep Throat' clashed', *The Washington Post*, 20 June, viewed 28 November 2013, www.washingtonpost.com.

Chapter 6

Incentives for blowing the whistle

The provision of financial rewards for whistleblowers exists solely in the United States, through the *False Claims Act* (FCA) and related legislation. Other countries have not adopted this concept. Those who argue against providing whistleblowers with compensation assert that we live predominately within an ethical society, and have a desire and preference to work within ethical institutions, and that such values are sufficient to motivate people to speak out against wrongdoing. If coupled with the assurances that the complaint will be dealt with, and that the whistleblower will be safe, they assert that people will be motivated sufficiently to speak out. They use terms such as informers, bounty hunters and the like to describe those who collect rewards for blowing the whistle.[1]

This chapter, for four reasons, argues to the contrary. The first is that the savings that the US government has made through its whistleblower rewards systems, as outlined below, are so massive that they pose an opportunity that is relevant to all countries. The second is that the FCA stops wrongdoing – the primary objective of any whistleblowing action. The third reason is that whistleblowers *do* suffer. A sound argument can be put forward that they should be compensated for the suffering that they have experienced in pushing for the stopping of wrongdoing. Although the FCA applies only to government procurement, the rewards it offers can still be considered as a compensation for the difficulties that the whistleblower went through. A fourth reason builds on a combination of the first and second. In fact, it can be argued that the stronger moral stance is to adopt a False Claims program. The savings to government are monies that could support the many social programs – in health, in education, in poverty alleviation – that governments fund. Instead, by not instituting such a program, these funds are being stolen by business organisations willing to cheat, for example, on their invoicing or tax returns.

The US initiated the 1863 *False Claims Act* at the time of the Civil War. It was designed to identify contractor claimants who had not supplied goods as had been contracted. Stories of sawdust instead of gunpowder or diseased mules are used to illustrate the reasons behind the legislation.

The FCA has provisions which originated in England in the 13th century as a way to enforce the King's laws. A person, termed a 'relator', could bring a *qui tam* suit – initially on behalf of the King – to prevent fraud against the government. The term is an abbreviation of the Latin phrase *qui tam pro domino rege quam pro se ipso in hac parte sequitur*, meaning '[he] who sues in this matter for the king as [well as] for himself'. This legislation had become obsolete in England by 1950.

The FCA in the US fell into disuse following changes in 1943 when the Attorney General at the time, Francis Biddle, argued that strengthened federal law enforcement legislation made 'informers' unnecessary. The revised Act reduced the incentives and put other obstacles in the way of the relator. The incidence of employee reporting of contractor corruption dropped noticeably as a result.

Biddle reflected views that are still prevalent today. With the rise in false claims that followed his actions, however, the Act was reconstituted in a series of amendments in 1986. Stephen Kohn, Executive Director of the National Whistleblowers Center, makes little effort to weigh the pros and cons of rewards for whistleblowers. He totally supports *qui tam* legislation. Kohn is also Attorney-Trustee for the National Whistleblower Legal Defense and Education Fund. In his book *The Whistleblower's Handbook: A Step-by-Step Guide to Doing What's Right and Protecting Yourself*, [2] he provides 21 rules for people thinking of blowing the whistle. Rule 2 is 'Follow the money' where he advises using the *qui tam* provisions of the *False Claims Act* as well as those other pieces of legislation which have *qui tam* clauses. Rule 7 of his list is 'Check for tax cheats, using the Internal Revenue Service *qui tam*'. Rule 8 is 'Know the Dodd Frank Securities and Commodities *qui tam* clauses'. Rule 18 of Kohn's book is 'Get every penny deserved'.

Kohn states that the *False Claims Act* 'has proven to be the most effective anti-fraud act in the United States and perhaps in the entire world'. He lists three other pieces of legislation that have *qui tam* capabilities:

- Section 406 of the Internal Revenue Code (2006) – for blowing the whistle on income tax fraud;
- Section 21 of the *Securities Exchange Act* – for exposing stock fraud and shareholder rip-offs, and includes the *Foreign Corrupt Practices Act*; and
- Section 23 of the *Commodities Exchange Act*, the part of Dodd Frank which covers commodity trading.

The FCA is also in the process of being extended to individual states. The *Deficit Reduction Omnibus Reconciliation Act* of 2005 provided financial incentives for states to adopt their own versions of the FCA. At least 24 states now have false claims statutes, with many focusing on health care. In addition, at least three cities and the District of Columbia have adopted versions of the FCA.

Under the FCA, a successful *qui tam* whistleblower can receive between 15 percent and 30 percent of the total amount of money recovered for the government (the rest goes back to the government). While the percentage might seem low, the monetary amounts can be very substantial. In part, this is because the *False Claims Act* provides for treble damages.

Are US *qui tam* provisions applicable to other countries?

The United Kingdom

This is one of the questions asked of the 2013 UK enquiry on the UK *Public Interest Disclosures Act*. The whistleblowers support group, Public Concern at Work (PCaW), inaugurated an inquiry in approaches to strengthening the Act. This inquiry, The Whistleblowing Commission, reported in November 2013. It recommended against a reward system in the United Kingdom. The Commission gave six reasons, stating that it:

1. was inconsistent with the culture and philosophy of the UK;
2. undermined the moral stance of a genuine whistleblower;
3. could lead to false or delayed reporting;
4. could undermine credibility of witnesses in future criminal or civil proceedings;
5. could result in the negative portrayal of whistleblowers; and
6. would be inconsistent with the current compensatory regime in the UK.

Some of these reasons appear to be restatements of a single reason – they negate the culture and the moral stance of the UK whistleblower. The moral position is not that obvious, however, as the ultimate position is that the wrongdoing is stopped, wrongdoing which is potentially depriving governments of very large revenues which could be used to finance vitally needed social programs.

In addition, reason 3 implies that a whistleblower should not reveal a wrongdoing until he or she has enough evidence to be convincing – a recommendation that later paragraphs recommend should be adopted by all whistleblowers if they wish their disclosures to instigate an investigation. Also, as evidenced in later chapters, including that on the UK, false reporting is a problem that afflicts many whistleblowing incidents.

A second inquiry by the Department for Business Innovation and Skills, the government department with responsibility for the *Public Interest Disclosures Act* in the UK, is unlikely to make any changes. PCaW was the organisation that originally instituted the *Public Interest Disclosures Act* through a private member's bill, and exerts a strong influence over whistleblowing matters in the UK.

The commission added some explanations and amplifications to the reasons that it gave. One was that there is no reason why whistleblowers should not be rewarded in other ways; a second was that there are already limited reward systems operating in the UK. Nevertheless, it is an unfortunate recommendation, as the remainder of this chapter illustrates.

Australia

This question has strong support in this country. The Australian Federal Police Association (AFPA) lobbied for the introduction of an Australian False Claims Act:

> *During the 2010 Federal Election, the AFPA sought a commitment from the major political parties to consider the introduction of a* Qui Tam *False Claims Bill for Australia to address fraud on the Commonwealth, in particular. Both major parties committed to consider the AFPA proposal.*[3]

The Tax Justice Network, an alliance of non-profit organisations that campaigns against tax havens and for tax reform, also wants Australia to adopt laws modelled on the *False Claims Act* in the US. Dr Mark Zirnsak, from the Network, has stated that the 1986 amendments had resulted in a dramatic spike in fraud detection in the US. Canada recently flagged it would adopt similar laws. Dr Zirnsak has said that there appeared to be a reluctance to introduce such rewards in Australia.[4]

The Australian Civil Liberty Union (ACLU) also advocates an Australian False Claims Act, describing it as: '*Qui Tam* ... taking action for the good of the community'.[5]

Implementing US-style anti-fraud laws in the Australian pharmaceutical and health care industries has the potential for large compensation payments. Thomas Faunce, Gregor Urbas and Lesley Skillen point out on the website of the Department of Health and Ageing that the Australian pharmaceutical market is unlikely to be immune from US-style false claims and fraud. The reason is that most of the major drug companies, previously proven to have engaged in such conduct against the US government, also dominate the Australian market. The Department website repeats the article written for the Medical Journal of Australia.[6]

Evidence that is available to determine whether the wrongs reported under whistleblowing arrangements in Australia might be alleviated by a False Claims type action depend on how much illegal procurement activity takes place in Australia. The Victorian Ombudsman, in his Annual Report for 2011/12, states: 'Procurement continues to be a matter of concern for my office and is regularly the subject of whistleblower investigations.'[7] Preventing the illegal or improper purchase of goods or services by the public sector is a key objective of the *False Claims Act*, and this would indicate that a similar Act in Australia would pay dividends.

A report by the University of Melbourne and KPMG estimated that the total amount of money lost to corporate fraud in Australia, including in the health care sector, was about A$350m in 2010, and that it was growing at an annual rate of seven percent, with only approximately a third being detected.[8]

A deeper examination into the benefits of a False Claims Act in Australia is provided by Dr Kim Sawyer of the School of Philosophical and Historical Inquiries at the University of Melbourne. Sawyer argues for a False Claims Act based on the increased probability of a successful prosecution, together with its lowered costs.[9] In short, it has a higher benefit–cost ratio than other whistleblowing legislation. Later chapters, which examine the difficulties of whistleblowing regulation worldwide, together with the lack of success in prosecutions for whistleblower retaliation – particularly in Australia – would add weight to this contention.

The savings that are possible

The principal argument for installing a False Claims Act in the UK and in Australia is the massive financial benefits that would be obtained. Fines and reparations levied against US companies have returned large sums to the US Treasury. Included are Glaxo Smith Kline – US$3b to settle whistleblower charges of kickbacks and for doctoring research; Pfizer – US$2.3b for fraudulent sales claims; Abbott Laboratories – US$1.5b; and Johnson & Johnson – US$158m. Department of Justice statistics show that, in 2012, it recovered US$3.3b in settlements and judgments under the whistleblower provisions of just the *False Claims Act*. Over US$40b was recovered through the legislation in the 25 years to September 2012.

These companies all operate in Australia and the UK. It is not unreasonable to expect that they would operate similarly in these two countries as in the US.

Although the bulk of the *qui tam* cases appear to apply to companies in the health care industry, such is not always the case. CA Technologies, formerly known as Computer Associates and CA Inc., recently agreed (November 2013) to pay US$11m to settle allegations that the company violated the federal and state *False Claims Acts* through fraudulent billing practices.

Other examples outside the health and pharmaceuticals industry can be found on the Department of Justice website. One example is of four student aid lenders paying a total of US$57m for improperly inflating their entitlement to interest rate subsidies from the US Department of Education. The whistleblower was a Dr Jon Oberg, a former employee of the Department.[10]

Perhaps the most noteworthy case in the US is that of Bradley Birkenfeld, who blew the whistle on UBS, the Swiss Bank, under the whistleblower provisions of the Internal Revenue Code. He was awarded US$104m as part of the settlement. UBS in 2009 agreed to turn over more than 4,000 US taxpayer account holders and to pay US$780m to resolve a criminal case involving secret offshore accounts (see Box 7: Whistleblower of the Century).

Since then, more than 33,000 US taxpayers have confessed to holding undeclared overseas accounts and have paid more than US$5b in taxes and penalties.

A strong argument in favour of a False Claims Act and associated financial legislation in the UK is a study by David Lewis, who determined that the most common form of wrongdoing in the first ten years of the *Public Interest Disclosures Act* in the UK was financial malpractice. Such wrongdoing is the prime objective of the recent legislation enacted in the United States.[11]

Possible developments

It seems highly likely that Australia, and perhaps the UK, will make a positive recommendation on adopting a version of the *False Claims Act* at some stage, although not in the immediate future. The benefits of this Act are too strong to be ignored. There will be some reluctance to make the recommendation, for it will be argued that those who speak out will do so only for the financial reward. Such a motivation negates the concept that a whistleblower also speaks out due to an innate desire to ensure openness and honesty.

Either country may wish to consider a suggestion that Dr Suelette Dreyfus put forward in a recent article – that instead of the whistleblower taking a *qui tam* action, he/she be awarded costs and compensation from a fund built up from the fines, or savings, from this and previous actions.[12] Dreyfus, thus, argues for a defence fund to cover legal costs. It could, however, be extended further to provide compensation for damages as well as costs.

[1] For a more complete history, see Harmon, A 2011, 'Bounty hunters and whistleblowers: Constitutional concerns for false claims actions after passage of the patient protection and affordable health care act of 2010', *Labor & Employment Law Forum*, vol. 2, issue 1, article 3. This Act is often described as Obamacare.
[2] Kohn, S 2011, *The whistleblowers handbook*, Lyons Press, Connecticut.
[3] The Federal Police continue to lobby for the introduction of this legislation. See Australian Federal Police Association 2012, Government continues to take seriously AFPA argument for a *Qui Tam* False Claims Bill for Australia, AFPA, ACT, viewed 1 October 2013, www.afpa.org.au/sites/default/files/publications/1085.pdf.
[4] Williams, R & Butler, B 2013, 'Push to give whistleblowers a cut', The Age, June 5, viewed 1 October 2013, www.theage.com.au.
[5] Posted on the ACLU website by its editorial team 2010, Qui tam … do we need it here?, Civil Liberties Australia, 27 December, viewed 10 October 2013, www.cla.asn.au/News/qui-tam-do-we-need/.
[6] Faunce T, Urbas G & Skillen L 2011, 'Implementing US-style anti-fraud laws in the Australian pharmaceutical and health care industries', Medical Journal of Australia, vol. 194, pp. 474-478.
[7] Victorian Ombudsman 2012, Annual report 2012, viewed 20 October 2013, p. 46, www.parliament.vic.gov.au/file_uploads/Victoria_Ombudsman_Annual_Report_2012_P1_7TsdZNMQ.PDF
[8] KPMG 2010, Fraud and misconduct survey 2010, Australia and New Zealand, KPMG, viewed 1 November 2013, www.kpmg.com/AU/en/IssuesAndInsights/ArticlesPublications/Fraud-Survey/Documents/Fraud-and-Misconduct-Survey-2010.pdf.
[9] Sawyer, K 2011, 'Lincoln's law. An analysis of an Australian False Claims Act', Social Sciences Research Network, viewed 7 March 2012.

[10] Department of Justice 2010, *Four Student Aid Lenders Settle False Claims Act Suit*, DOJ, Washington, 17 November, viewed November 20 2013, www.justice.gov.

[11] Lewis, D 2010, 'Ten years of Public Interest Disclosure Act, 1998 claims, What can we learn from the statistics and recent research?', *Industrial Law Journal*, vol 3, no. 3, p. 326.

[12] Dreyfus, S 2013, 'Keeping us honest: protecting whistleblowers', *The Conversation,* web log post, 2 April, viewed 20 May 2013, http://theconversation.com/keeping-us-honest-protecting-whistleblowers-13131.

Box 6: The European Commission

Paul van Buitenen, Whistleblower

Paul van Buitenen, in 1999, was suspended on half pay while disciplinary action was launched against him. Van Buitenen, a Dutch citizen, was assistant auditor in the European Commission's Internal Audit Unit. He had become concerned about fraud within the Commission's Leonardo da Vinci programme (on vocational education). He had been suspended for informing the European Parliament about his concerns. He had thought it vital for the Parliament to make informed decisions on the programme's budget and had therefore decided in late 1998 to inform the Parliament directly. He relied on an article in staff regulations which enabled staff to go against instructions if the Commission's administration had been properly notified previously and if the instructions breach criminal law.[1]

The Leonardo programme was his particular responsibility, but in discussions with auditors in other fields he found similar irregularities elsewhere in the Commission. He wrote a series of notes, complying with a staff regulation that required him to report concerns internally.

In March 1998, he was told that he had informed his superiors sufficiently of the irregularities and that he was discharged from any further obligation to report. He replied that, as a loyal official and a Christian, he considered himself never discharged from such an obligation. He made repeated requests to his superiors to adapt the audit of the Leonardo programme to take account of the evidence of fraud. These requests were rejected.

The Parliament asked a Committee of Independent Experts to look into his allegations. In March 1999 it published a report which fundamentally upheld van Buitenen's allegations, finding 'undoubted instances of fraud and corruption' within the Commission.[2] The most press-worthy revelation proved to be that a Commissioner, Edith Cresson, had appointed her friend, a dentist, to a post of Scientific Adviser for which he was manifestly unqualified. The next day the Commission, under Jacques Santer, resigned *en bloc*. Officials were also heavily criticised, although only three were dismissed.[3]

In April 1999, van Buitenen was transferred from Brussels to a new low profile job in Luxembourg. He wrote a book about his experiences[4] and, in 2001, the new Commission granted him two months off work to complete a full report on his allegations. This report was submitted but has not been published. He eventually resigned when it became clear to him that no effective reforms had followed. He came to the conclusion that the Commission was inherently unreformable as long as it was not subject to democratic control. He turned to political life and was elected as a member of the European Parliament from 2004-09. He has continued to uncover malpractice in the Commission, and now, as a Dutch MP, is campaigning for better treatment for whistleblowers.

He was named 'European of the Year' by Reader's Digest magazine and the Australian Broadcasting Commission.

Source: Paul Stephenson.

---

[1] The current version of this regulation is 21a of the EC Staff Regulations 2004
[2] First Report on allegations regarding fraud, mismanagement and nepotism in the European Commission, 19.3.1999
[3] OJ C81 E/38 13.3.2001
[4] Blowing the Whistle (Politicos) 2000

Chapter 7

Regulatory failure

Widespread evidence would suggest that in most countries the investigative process is less than fully effective. This chapter outlines the research findings, so far, that can be brought to bear on this question, and then suggests approaches for further analysis that will hopefully lead to eventual resolution. It also suggests steps by which the whistleblower can support and strengthen the investigatory process.

The United States

The *Sarbanes Oxley Act* in the US (SOX) was passed in 2002 to avert the financial crises of the type seen in the Tyco, WorldCom and Enron failures in the early part of that decade. It has since been widely considered a failure. Although whistleblowers came forward, none were convincing enough to stir the regulatory agencies into action on the financial institutions that brought on the global financial crisis (GFC) of 2007 and 2008.

The subsequent paragraphs document SOX failures, and then set out the evidence for regulatory failure generally.

Richard Moberley, an academic lawyer who has written and researched extensively on US whistleblower legislation, claimed that Sarbanes-Oxley's greatest lesson can be derived from its two most prominent failings. Firstly, over the past decade, the Act did not protect whistleblowers from suffering retaliation. Secondly, despite SOX, whistleblowers did not play a significant role in uncovering the financial crisis that led to the GFC.[1] He and several other sources claim that whistleblowers did come forward – but that they achieved little. The

PBS documentary, the 'Untouchables' questioned why, five years after Lehman Bros filed for bankruptcy, not one major Wall Street executive has been prosecuted for fraud tied to the sale of bad mortgages.[2]

The Ponzi scheme of Bernie Madoff also had a whistleblower (Harry Markopolos). He repeatedly warned the Securities and Exchange Commission (SEC) about Madoff – yet again his actions had no impact.[3]

A number of studies have asserted that the process of accepting and investigating a whistleblower disclosure is less than efficient. The following paragraphs outline several: 1. The Securities Exchange Commission (SEC 2009); 2. Dworkin (2010); 3. Government Accountability Office audits (GAO) (2010); 4. the National Institute of Health (NIH) inquiry; 5. Nielsen (2013); and 6. the Ethics Resource Center (2013).

1. The SEC 2009

The 450-page SEC report, released September 2009, outlines a series of fumbles in which SEC staff failed to follow up on complaints. In the case involving Bernie Madoff, it wrongly accepted confusing and inconsistent answers to questions, or in some cases involved junior staff who didn't understand options-trading or Ponzi schemes.[4]

2. Dworkin 2010

Terry Morehead Dworkin, another well-known whistleblower researcher, explains the rationale for the *Sarbanes Oxley Act* 2002 and then sets out evidence of its failure. She also suggests that, in relation to the *False Claims Act*, this successful whistleblowing law still has significant problems. Dworkin concludes that there is only an illusion of protection, and that whistleblowers need help looking after themselves.[5]

3. GAO 2010

The GAO audits of the Occupational Safety and Health Administration were used by Moberly to strengthen support for his own conclusions:

> In 2009 and 2010, these conclusions received some support from two Government Accountability Office (GAO) independent audits of OSHA's whistleblower program. These audits found that OSHA lacked resources to investigate whistleblower claims adequately and that OSHA's investigators often lacked training to investigate complex cases.[6]

4. NIH

The NIH study interviewed 135 NIH investigators who reported research wrongdoing. They examined a variety of investigator actions, including reporting to the parent institution, peer shaming, and one-on-one discussions with the researcher. The study reached the conclusion that, at least in research organisations, considerable mismanagement of the investigations into the reported wrongdoing can be observed.[7]

5. Nielsen 2013

Nielsen draws on an extensive review of the research literature to identify four obstacles to effective whistleblowing. Three of the four are related to ineffective regulation. These are (i) lack of staff; (ii) underskilled staff; and (iii) political pressure not to investigate. The fourth obstacle to effective whistleblowing is the direct risk to the whistleblower.

6. Ethics Resource Center 2013

Another example worth noting is an Ethics Resource Center study on whistleblower hotlines. It lends weight to the conclusion that whistleblowing systems are facing difficulty in achieving full administrative impact.[8] The study covered 612 complainants in five companies, and included grievance complaints as well as wrongdoing complaints. Undertaken in 2013, the study found that, of the 612 complainants, 38 percent of the reports did not stand up under initial scrutiny by ethics officials and were effectively dismissed without further action. Only 21 percent were fully substantiated. The others were referred by ethics officials to the appropriate unit for additional inquiry. With only 21 percent fully substantiated, the study suggests that either the majority of whistleblower disclosures were not meeting the regulators' requirements, or the regulators were dismissing complainants with little or no effort to investigate further.

The United Kingdom

United Kingdom findings are less clear cut, primarily because the appropriate research, as outlined above for the US, has not yet been undertaken. Under the current system, the majority of whistleblowers can go directly to a regulator, of which there are about 45. However, there are no studies on how many of those disclosures are dealt with. If the whistleblower complains to his/her employing organisation and experiences discrimination, he or she can go to an Employment Tribunal. At the Employment Tribunal, the whistleblower is awarded job restitution and/or such damages as the Tribunal deems appropriate.

A large percentage of submissions are settled out of the Tribunal in a confidential agreement. An article by Cathy James, Director of Public Concern at Work (PCaW) , the non-government organisation supporting whistleblowers, claims that overall this means an outsider, including PCaW, can see information about the whistleblower's concern in only five percent of all PIDA claims.[9] There is correspondingly little information on whether the wrong was stopped.

In a review by the UK Department for Business Innovation and Skills (DBIS) , the National Association of Schoolmasters supported James' claim, asserting that wrongdoing is currently being 'hushed up' in 70 percent of public interest disclosures.[10] In other words, companies at the receiving end of the complaint are able to buy off the whistleblowers. DBIS has since instituted a procedure by which the documentation of the whistleblower's complaint is sent to the appropriate regulator, provided the whistleblower agrees. The whistleblower has to tick a question on the Employment Tribunal application form (the ET1 form), saying he/she is willing for his/her form to be sent to the appropriate regulator. The ET1 Form is a 16-page application for compensation and redress on a range of employment issues, including retaliation. It is not a notification of a wrongdoing. Earlier sections in this chapter indicate that whistleblowing investigations are not particularly successful, even when the whistleblower has the opportunity to provide full details of the wrongdoing. It is, therefore, unlikely that a tick on such a form will activate many investigations.

David Lewis points out yet another issue in the question of regulatory investigation in the UK. A worker who has revealed a wrongdoing by their organisation, whether real or imagined, is dismissed or otherwise experiences retaliation by that employer, and is then offered a settlement during the course of an employment tribunal investigation. It would be difficult to reject such an offer. Lewis describes a worker who would give up such a settlement as altruistic.[11]

The Whistleblowing Commission recently reviewed the effectiveness of the British *Protected Disclosures Act*, including the new system for handling the investigation and regulation. PCaW sponsored the enquiry, outlined in the previous chapter. An inquiry by the Department for Business Innovation and Skills (DBIS) is also underway. This author's assessment, prior to this inquiry, was that the regulator would need more information and a possible interview with the whistleblower if it were to resolve any issue that does not have clearly available evidence to support the whistleblower's complaint. This aspect of the investigation into wrongdoing is included under the terms of reference of both the PCaW and DBIS inquiries. The Commission found that: 'The majority of respondents did not think that regulators make adequate use of the information that they receive from whistleblowers.'[12]

The findings coming out of the Commission in this respect are contained in Recommendations 4 and 5:

> *Recommendation 4: The Commission recommends that regulators have a clear procedure for dealing with whistleblowers…*
>
> *Recommendation 5: The Commission recommends that regulators include whistleblowing in their annual reporting mechanisms … The information … should include:*
> a) *the number and type of concerns received by regulators from whistleblowers;*
> b) *the number of enforcement actions that have been triggered or contributed to by whistleblowers;*
> c) *the number of PIDA claims that have been referred by the employment tribunal services;*
> d) *the number of organisations which failed to have in place effective whistleblowing arrangements and what action was taken as a result; and*

e)   *what action has been taken to promote and enforce the Code.*

Some of this information is vital if the effectiveness of the regulatory process in the UK is to be assessed. Currently it is not known how and to what extent regulators enforce organisations to correct wrongdoings exposed by whistle-blowers. It is not even known how many whistleblowing disclosures are received and acted upon. Such research is necessary.

James also claims that the statistics coming out of the tribunal system show that eight out of ten concerns are first raised with an employer.[13] Some eight percent go directly to a regulator. She states that these are not official figures but are drawn from PCaW research into PIDA judgments. That eight out of ten go to their employer first is consistent with figures from other countries. The percentage of complainants who go to a tribunal is unknown. However, if 70 percent of the whistleblower complaints end in out-of-tribunal settlements, then the numbers that end with a regulator for investigation and action are small.

Australia

Australia has only recently introduced a national whistleblower protection program for its Federal civil servants. Any assessment of achievement therefore can only be made against the various pieces of state legislation, each of which has a Public Interest Disclosures or Whistleblower Protection Act. The following sample of three states and one territory (there are six states and two territories in total) paint a scattered picture, which is generally supportive of the contention that investigations present less than a full picture of total effectiveness.

The Victorian Ombudsman reported in its 2012 Annual report that it had received 117 disclosures, of which 79 were neither public interest disclosures (PIDs) nor protected disclosures (the distinction was not made clear). Thirty eight were investigated.[14] The outcomes of the 38 investigated were not documented.

The Queensland Ombudsman reports show that the outcomes of the PID investigations were:

- 43.2 percent substantiated (290 PIDs)
- 5.2 percent partially substantiated (35 PIDs)
- 48.5 percent unsubstantiated (326 PIDs).

It is not known why almost half the PIDs were unsubstantiated, or why a substantial number of PIDs were not even checked. In 2012/13 1,140 PIDs were reported in Queensland. This represented a four percent decrease on the previous year.[15]

In the Northern Territory, the whistleblowing authority is the Office of the Commissioner for Public Interest Disclosures. Its annual report for 2011/12 indicated:

- Actual disclosures   2010/11   75
- Estimated   2011/12   60

- Actual   2011/12   70
- Target   2012/13   60

The Commissioner reported that 65 percent were investigated within six months. The Annual Report also noted that it employed a second investigator during the year and a number of consultants. One investigation took six person months to complete.[16] Of 41 disclosures made during the reporting year, 32 were assessed and ultimately rejected by the Commissioner on the grounds that they were not matters attracting the protections of the Act.

- five disclosures were accepted as public interest disclosures, attracting the protections of the Act, and were investigated and completed;
- four were assessed and referred to another body for investigation.

Of the 32 disclosures ultimately rejected by the Commissioner:

- 59 percent were assessed as not involving improper conduct as defined by the Act;
- 13 percent were unable to be assessed due to insufficient information being provided or obtainable;
- 13 percent had already been adequately investigated;
- nine percent were assessed as personal or employment-related grievances;
- three percent were assessed as allegations about policy decisions of a public body or public officer that they were not entitled to make; and
- three percent were outside the jurisdiction of this office as the alleged improper conduct did not concern a public officer or public body.

On 20 October 2011, the Western Australia (WA) Parliament introduced the *Evidence and Public Interest Disclosure Legislation Amendment Bill* 2011 (WA) to amend the *Evidence Act* 1906 (WA) and the *Public Interest Disclosure Act* 2003 (WA) with the purpose of granting so-called 'shield laws' for journalists and public sector whistleblowers. The legislation was passed in September 2012. The Ombudsman in Western Australia reports on all complaints it receives without separating out the public interest disclosures. It is not possible, therefore, to check the effectiveness of the *Public Interest Disclosure Act*.

Examining Australia in general, a reasonable conclusion can be drawn from the above performance data that the investigative process in the whistleblowing systems in the Australian states may not be particularly effective. A supporting reason for reaching this conclusion is the low utilisation of the retaliation provisions. There have been no prosecutions by an Australian integrity agency for retaliation since the Acts were first initiated.

A third reason, again still not conclusive, is that effective management of whistleblowing protection in the public sector faces considerable difficulty. This is a distinct whistleblowing issue that has implications for all countries, and is treated separately in a later section.

In further work on their 2008 survey of whistleblowing in Australia[17] Roberts, Brown and Olsen undertook a series of interviews with 16 national, state and local agencies. They note that the current standard of investigations conducted by public sector organisations is perceived to be low.[18] Their study is on internal whistleblowing, but for the reasons discussed below, internal and external regulatory failure, in some aspects, portray interlinked difficulties.

Reasons why regulation may not be successful

Conclusions drawn from the above examples would suggest that the investigative processes in all three countries face difficulties. This section outlines four possible reasons why:

1. Insufficient numbers or skills in investigative resources.

    This is the conclusion reached by Moberly. He states: '*Two primary factors contributed to the difficulties whistleblowers had winning cases: administrative recalcitrance and adjudicative hamstringing.*'[19]

    His assessment was that the low percentage of complaints that were managed effectively was due to administrative weaknesses and excessively rigorous legal interpretations. This may be the actual reasons, but other explanations are possible. Vaughn likewise commented negatively on the activities of the Office of the Special Counsel (OSC) created by the whistleblower provisions of the *Civil Service Reform Act* of 1978: 'From the beginning, the office was understaffed and lacked adequate resources'.[20] Later, he adds that the problem is wider than inadequate resources, extending to adequate management of the investigative process '…the OSC failed not only to fulfil the loftiest of expectations, but also to meet more modest ones'.[21]

2. The complaint does not meet legislative requirements. The dismissal of a number of the Australian complaints as not being protected disclosures does suggest that the complaint is one that is not identified in the legislation.

3. The complaint contains little more than unsupported accusations. The disclosure may not have enough detail to warrant an investigation. Alternatively, the accusation could have possibly been made from a person with an unbalanced or biased viewpoint toward the organisation or his/her superior officer. The regulator assesses the disclosure as such and decides not to investigate. Many readers who work in whistleblowing will, on occasions, receive an email or letter, usually of excessive length, and often repetitive, that signals that the sender is obsessed by the problem that he or she is complaining about. It can reasonably be assumed that some of the disclosures dismissed by the investigating bodies would exhibit these reasons.

4. The nature of a bureaucratic response. This is one of the conclusions reached by Nielsen's examination of the reasons for investigative weaknesses.[22] Nielsen quotes the classic texts on bureaucracy (Max

Weber), and the need for established procedures. This reason can be taken a little further in exploring the nature of a public sector examination. Regulators, who will be employed by the agency responsible for the sector on which the whistle has been blown, are necessarily cautious. They are not willing to act unilaterally without outside support for a decision which may be controversial. Many, if not most whistleblowing cases, pit the whistleblower's story against that of the parent organisation. The employing organisation will deny the accusation if it possibly can. The regulating agency seeks to find out which story is the correct one. It either contracts out the investigation, or asks another civil service agency to determine what happened. If no clear answer is provided, the agency will just let the matter fade, and nothing will happen.

Conclusion

The findings of this chapter certainly indicate that there are problems with assessing and dealing with whistleblower complaints. More research is needed, research that would certainly be assisted by whistleblower authorities providing a fuller picture of their activities. At minimum, each should provide sufficient information to assess the nature of the complaints received, and their performance in dealing with those complaints. This information would include: (i) the number of disclosures received; (ii) the number not investigated; (iii) the reasons why they were not investigated; (iv) the conclusions reached on those that were investigated; and (v) actions taken.

It is of vital importance that we undertake the research to develop a clearer picture of how effectively regulators are dealing with the information sent to them. It will, then, be possible to set up compensatory systems. Until we have that picture, a whistleblower's disclosure must be sufficient to convince the regulator to undertake an investigation. Such information would comprise full details of the wrongdoing, where it complies with the relevant Act, what is the supporting evidence, and who will corroborate all or part of this evidence.

---

[1] Moberly, R 2012, 'Sarbanes-Oxley's whistleblower provisions – ten years later', *Social Science Research Network*, May 21, viewed 1 November 2013, http://ssrn.com/abstract=2064061.

[2] Breslow, J 2013, *Is Wall Street Still "Untouchable"?*, PBS, May 21, viewed, November 10 2013, www.pbs.org.

[3] Morrissey, J 2009, 'SEC Internal Review Cites Multiple Failures on Madoff', *Time Magazine*, 2 September.

[4] Ibid

[5] Dworkin, T 2010, 'US whistleblowing: a decade of progress?' in D Lewis (ed.), A Global Approach to Public Interest Disclosure: what can we learn from existing whistleblowing legislation and research, Edward Elgar, Cheltenham, UK.

[6] Government Accountability Office 2010, Whistleblower protection sustained management attention needed to address long-standing program weaknesses, GAO, August 2010, Washington, DC.

[7] Sieber, J 2012, 'Witnesses to Research wrongdoing', Journal of Empirical Research on Human Research Ethics, vol. 7, no. 5, pp. 3-14.

[8] Ethics Resource Centre 2013, Encouraging employee reporting through procedural justice, ERC, viewed 6 June 2013, www.ethics.org/files/u5/procedural-justice.pdf.

[9] James, C 2011, 'Whistleblowing, risk and regulation', in D Lewis & W Vandekerckhove (eds.), *Whistleblowing and democratic values,* Proceedings of the International whistleblowing research network 2011, Middlesex University, London, 23-24 June 2011, *viewed 2 November 2013* p.117, http://academia.edu/1348441/Whistleblowing_and_Democratic_Values_free_ebook.

[10] Department for Business, Innovation & Skills 2010, *Government response – employment tribunal claims and the Public Interest Disclosure Act*, DBIS, January, viewed 15 December 2013, p. 5, www.berr.gov.uk/files/file54221.pdf.

[11] Lewis, D 2010, 'Ten years of Public Interest Disclosure Act, 1998 Claims. What can we learn from the statistics and recent research?' *Industrial Law Journal,* vol. 3, no. 3, p. 327.

[12] The Whistleblowing Commission 2013, Report on the effectiveness of existing arrangements for workplace whistleblowing in the UK, PCaW, November, viewed 29 December 2013, p.10, www.pcaw.org.uk/files/WBC percent20Report percent20Final.pdf.

[13] James, *op cit.,* p.119.

[14] Victorian Ombudsman 2012, *Annual report 2012*, viewed 2 December, p. 43, www.parliament.vic.gov.au/file_uploads/Victoria_Ombudsman_Annual_Report_2012_P1_7Ts dZNMQ.PDF.

[15] Queensland Ombudsman 2013, *Annual report, 2012 – 13,* viewed 2 December, p.61, www.ombudsman.qld.gov.au/Portals/0/docs/Publications/Annual_Reports/2012-13 percent20
AnnualReport_FINAL_12.9.13_V2.pdf.

[16] Office of the Commissioner for Public Interest Disclosures, Northern Territory, Annual report 2011 /12, viewed December 2, 2013.p.7, www.blowthewhistle.nt.gov.au/publications/ documents/annual percent20report percent202012-13 percent20.pdf.

[17] Brown, AJ (ed.) 2008, *Whistleblowing in the Australian public sector. Enhancing the theory and practice of internal witness management in public sector organisations,* ANU E Press, Canberra.

[18] Roberts, P, Brown, AJ & Olsen, J 2011, *Whistling while they work,* ANU E Press, Canberra, p.62.

[19] Moberley, op cit., p.28.

[20] Vaughn, R 2013, Successes and failures of whistleblower laws, Edward Elgar, Cheltenham, UK, p. 170.

[21] Ibid, p.176.

[22] Nielsen, R 2012, 'Whistle-blowing methods for navigating within and helping reform regulatory institutions,' *Journal of Business Ethics,* vol.112, no 3, pp.385-395.

Box 7: Whistleblower of the Century

Bradley Birkenfeld, Whistleblower

'Whistleblower of the century' is the title given to Bradley Birkenfeld by FAIR – the Federal Accountability Initiative for Reform, a whistleblower support group active in Canada.[1] Birkenfeld's disclosures in 2007 provided data to the United States Department of Justice that resulted in $780m in fines being levied against the Swiss banking company UBS. Birkenfeld was the 'go-between' between UBS, his employer, and the bank's US-based clients wishing to hide taxable income. Birkenfeld, who was charged with and pleaded guilty to conspiracy to defraud the United States, was sentenced in 2009 to 40 months in prison.

The Internal Revenue Service (IRS) paid Birkenfeld a $104m award in September 2012 for acting as a corporate whistleblower under the *Dodd Frank Act*.

Birkenfeld began working for UBS in Geneva in 2001. His principal responsibility was to solicit wealthy Americans to invest in the bank and, thus, avoid paying US taxes. Although UBS was not permitted to give investment advice in the US, the bank instructed Birkenfeld and similar employees to lie about the purpose of their trips to the US. Birkenfeld advised American clients how to avoid scrutiny, including placing cash and jewels in Swiss safe deposit boxes.

A 2009 Time magazine article states that no one, including Birkenfeld himself, would argue that Bradley Birkenfeld, 42 at the time of his disclosures, was a saint.[2] The former UBS banking executive hasn't hidden the fact that he once bought diamonds with illicit money in Europe and then spirited them to California stuffed in a toothpaste tube, all part of an effort to conceal $200m in assets on which his client — the Russia-born, California-based real estate mogul Igor Olenicoff — owed $7.2m in US taxes. But at the same time, almost no one in the US government would deny that Birkenfeld was absolutely essential to its landmark tax evasion case against the Swiss banking giant UBS.

The jailing of Birkenfeld raised much criticism. Various advocacy organizations around the world requested that Attorney General Eric Holder review Birkenfeld's case. A letter from the National Whistleblowers Center said that the 'destructive impact of Mr Birkenfeld's sentencing will radically undermine the ability of law enforcement to detect, prosecute and prevent illegal off-shore banking practices'.[3]

The Make it Safe Coalition, a bipartisan coalition of leading advocacy groups, awarded Bradley Birkenfeld with its 'Tax Whistleblower of the Year' presentation at the 2010 National Whistleblower Assembly. At the time Birkenfeld was still in prison, but he was released in 2012 after serving thirty months – some of it in home detention.

The charging of Birkenfeld raises complex issues. There is no doubt that his own actions were illegal, and that his charging and sentencing were correct. But the advocacy groups agitating for his release had a solid case. Birkenfeld had stopped massive fraud. His imprisonment would only discourage future whistleblowers involved in wrongdoing from coming forward.

In 2009, Switzerland amended its secrecy on federal banking laws, often seen as a haven for illicit money, as a result of Birkenfeld's whistleblowing.

---

[1] Federal Accountability Initiative for Reform – Protecting Whistleblowers Who Protect The Public Interest Whistleblower of the Century? fairwhistleblower.ca. Viewed September 10 2013.
[2] Time Magazine . October 6,2009 Why Is the UBS Whistle-Blower Headed to Prison? www.time.com/time/business/article viewed Novemeber 2013.
[3] 'International and National Advocacy Organizations Urge Attorney General Holder to Investigate Birkenfeld Case'. *WebWire*. November 25, 2009.

Chapter 8

The United States

One of the objectives of this book is to assist whistleblowers in getting their message across without damage to themselves and, initially at least, through their own efforts, without requiring extensive legal assistance. However, the number and complexity of the different legislative acts in the US makes this a next-to-impossible task. There are over fifty separate pieces of legislation at the Federal level alone. *Qui tam* legislation that pays rewards to whistleblowers applies in four different US Federal Acts, and in about half the states of the United States.[1] Separate whistleblower legislation of varying quality has been established in all states. This complexity leads Stephen Kohn, Attorney and Trustee for the National Whistleblower Center, to argue for greater simplicity in the US system: 'To this date, Congress has not passed a comprehensive national whistleblower law.'[2]

And a little later:

> *If you are going to blow the whistle, you must understand the complex maze of federal and state laws that govern your conduct, and ensure that you obtain the maximum legal protection.*[3]

Our first piece of advice on whistleblower safety is to identify and understand the legislation that protects you. It is outlined in Chapter 5, but it can become a difficult task when one is faced with this level of complexity. What this chapter can do, however, is steer the potential whistleblower towards those sources of information that can help him or her sort out what they can do. It should give the whistleblower enough information to make an initial decision on whether they should or should not blow the whistle.

This chapter will also provide sufficient information for ethics teachers and trainers to develop a program that can cover US systems in the classroom or workplace. It also provides background for those researching whistleblowing practices in their own countries, enabling them to judge the strengths and weaknesses of the US systems and what might be applicable in their own countries.

The Federal Government and the private sector

With the exception of the *False Claims Act* of 1863, the history of Federal Government legislation in the US started with the incorporation of whistleblower provisions in the *Occupational Safety and Health Act* in the Department of Labor in 1970. This Act legislated against any person being discriminated against for non-compliance with the Act. Several other private sector whistleblowing provisions were placed in various Acts over the next decade – Solid Waste Disposal, Toxic Substances Control, Surface Mining Control, Safe Drinking Water, Clean Air, etc. As noted, at the time of writing, there are over 50 Acts providing whistleblowing protection.

It has been an unfortunate development, for it becomes difficult for an ordinary worker in a company or industry to identify which law is providing protection. He or she may encounter a safety issue, or perhaps an environmental issue in, for example, the mining industry. It will require considerable searching to find out to whom they should report and how they are protected. For instance, occupational health and safety issues can arise in activities covered by many Acts. The *Surface Transportation Assistance Act* 1982, the *Asbestos Hazard Emergency Response Act* 1982, the *International Safety Container Act* of 1977, *Energy Reorganization Act*; and the *Clean Air Act* of 1977 are only some examples.

The *Sarbanes Oxley Act* and the *Dodd Frank Act*

In response to the meltdown in the previous decade of companies such as Enron, WorldCom, Tyco International, etc., the US passed the *Sarbanes Oxley Act* (SOX) in 2002 – also called the *Corporate and Criminal Fraud Accountability Act*. SOX requires that public companies provide secure reporting of accounting irregularities. Protection for whistleblowers who exposed contraventions of this Act was also part of SOX. Retaliation against a whistleblower results in reinstatement of the whistleblower, back pay, and legal fees. SOX also has severe criminal penalties – up to 10 years in prison – that can be levied on those found to have retaliated against a whistleblower.

The Act places additional reporting conditions and stronger financial controls on US corporations, and also requires companies to establish internal whistleblowing systems. When it was first introduced, SOX was hailed as a major legislative step forward:

> *Given its diverse civil, criminal and administrative provisions, the statute may be considered, over time, one of the most important whistleblower protection laws.*[4]

It was copied, at least in part, in upwards of a dozen other countries, including Australia, although not the UK.

The *Sarbanes Oxley Act*, however, has since been widely considered as a failure, as discussed in the previous chapter. The failure of SOX resulted in the passage of the *Dodd Frank Act* (*The Dodd-Frank Wall Street Reform and Consumer Protection Act* of 2010). This Act introduced a major change – it incorporated elements of the reward provisions of the *False Claims Act*. It also extended these reward provisions to other Acts protecting the financial services industry. Included were the Internal Revenue, Commodities Exchange and the Securities Exchange Acts. A concise guide to the various Federal legislation is available in Shimabukuro and Whitaker's *Whistleblower Protections Under Federal Law: An Overview*.[5]

Unlike Dodd-Frank, Sarbanes-Oxley did not offer a financial reward for whistleblowing.

Whistleblowing and anti-trust

For the first time, the Senate Judiciary Committee approved the creation of whistleblower protections for employees who report antitrust violations. At the time of writing, 2013, Congress is currently considering a Criminal Antitrust Anti-Retaliation Act. This Act would do the following:

1. Protect employees who report violations of antitrust laws internally, or to the Federal Government, from retaliation.

2. Allow employees to file a whistleblower retaliation claim with the Department of Labor. It would also grant a *de novo* review and a jury trial in Federal Court.

3. Provide employees who suffer retaliation to receive reinstatement, back pay, special damages, attorney's fees and costs.

According to the National Whistleblowers Center, this bill is a major step forward in plugging a loophole in the patchwork of whistleblower protection that currently exists.[6]

Government employee whistleblowing

The first legislation enacted to provide protection to Federal employees was the *Civil Service Reform Act* of 1978 (CSRA). It was the first in the English-speaking world to introduce whistleblowing provisions for civil servants. By comparison, the first such statute was introduced in Australia in 1994 and in the UK in 1998. Personal actions which discriminate among employees on marital status, political activity, or political affiliation were prohibited. Federal employees may file complaints regarding possible violations of this rule with the Office of Special Counsel (OSC), which was created as part of the Merit Services Protection Board.

They adjudicated on appeals by Federal employees who had been dismissed. Both offices still exist, the OSC being the arm of the government which hears whistleblower complaints. The Merit Services Protection Board was established to enhance and protect the quality of the US civil service. It guards against partisan political and other prohibited personnel practices, and against abuses by agency management.

Since 1978, most US states have enacted statutes protecting public employee whistleblowers. The CSRA was followed by the US *Whistleblower Protection Act* 1989. The most recent protection for public sector whistleblowers was the *Whistleblower Protection Enhancement Act*, passed into legislation by President Obama in November 2012.

The new legislation was designed to further protect Federal employees from reprisals (in addition to existing protections): if they are not the first person to disclose misconduct, if they disclose misconduct to co-workers or supervisors, if they disclose the consequences of a policy decision, or if they blow the whistle while carrying out their job duties.

Federal employees are protected from reprisal if they disclose: misconduct that evidences any violation of law, rule or regulation; mismanagement, a gross waste of funds, or an abuse of authority; or a substantial and specific danger to public health or safety.

The *Whistleblower Protection Enhancement Act* has not had sufficient time for its effectiveness to be assessed, but Nielsen has suggested that it too may not be effective.[7] Also, as discussed in a later chapter, providing effective protection for whistleblowers in the public sector and effective investigation regulation faces major hurdles.

Reward provisions

The protective provisions of the Dodd-Frank legislation will not be extended to whistleblowers if they raise their concerns internally rather than by contacting the Securities and Exchange Commission (SEC). Employees may bypass any internal company procedures and head straight for the SEC. As a result of this requirement, firms will have less scope to perform a pre-emptive internal investigation. Once the SEC commences an investigation, the degree of control that can be exercised by the company in respect of any internal investigation is reduced.

Additionally, foreign employees cannot take advantage of the US system. A recent case, Asadi v GE Energy (USA) LLC, specified that the Dodd-Frank anti-dismissal provisions will not extend to non-US citizens working in foreign jurisdictions for US companies.[8]

In summary

The US has, without doubt, the most comprehensive whistleblowing legislation and associated administrative systems in the Western world. They are also largely successful, although with the limitations previously noted. The legislation, however, is too complex to negotiate without legal assistance. Therefore, it does not readily meet the criterion of enabling everyday employees to safely speak out against wrongdoing. The National Whistleblowers Center is currently mounting a petition for a National Whistleblower Protection Act to redress this weakness.

> *Take Action! The absence of a comprehensive National Whistleblower Protection Act has resulted in serious loopholes in protection. This creates major hardship for honest employees who speak the truth to prevent disaster, only to learn that their government has let them down.*[9]

As discussed in the following chapter, Britain has just one law to cover everybody. As such, it is much simpler to use. It recently underwent one review by the Whistleblowing Commission, an investigative body set up by Public Concern at Work, the whistleblowing NGO that was instrumental is facilitating the original passage of the legislation in the United Kingdom. The efficacy of the British legislation, with the proposed amendments, is assessed in that chapter.

---

[1] National Whistleblowers Center n.d., *State qui tam laws,* NWC, *viewed 15 November 2013,* www.whistleblowers.org

[2] Kohn, S 2011, *The whistleblowers handbook,* Lyons Press, Connecticut, p.3.

[3] *ibid*, p.3

[4] Kohn, S n.d., Sarbanes-Oxley Act: *Legal Protection for Corporate Whistleblowers*, National Whistleblower Center, viewed 1 November 2013, www.whistelblowers.org.

[5] Shimabukuro, JO & Whitaker, LP 2012, *Whistleblower protections under Federal law: An overview,* Federal Publications, Cornell University, 13 September, viewed December 3 2013, http://digitalcommons.ilr.cornell.edu/key_workplace/945/.

[6] The National Whistleblowers Center n.d., *Pass the criminal antitrust anti-retaliation act*, NWC, viewed December 3 2013, www.whistleblowers.org, urging its members to contact their congressman.

[7] Nielsen, R 2012, Whistle-blowing methods for navigating within and helping reform regulatory institutions, *Journal of Business Ethics*, vol. 112, no. 3.

[8] Sprinzen, N 2012, The diminished scope Of Dodd-Frank whistleblower protections after Asadi v. G.E. Energy (USA), LLC, *The Metropolitan Corporate Counsel*, vol.20, no. 10.

[9] National Whistleblowers Center n.d., *Pass a national whistleblower protection act!*, NWC, viewed 17 November 2013, www.whistleblowers.org.

Box 8: The National Health Service

Gary Walker, Whistleblower

In 2009, Gary Walker was Chief Executive of the National Health Service's (NHS) trust responsible for Lincoln County Hospital in the UK. He was sacked in 2010 for 'gross professional misconduct' over alleged swearing at a meeting. Walker said he was forced to quit after refusing to meet Whitehall targets for non-emergency patients. He was concerned that medical staff had become accustomed to endangering patients' safety in order to accommodate them in overstretched hospitals. His solution was to cancel non-urgent operations to make adequate space for emergency patients.

There was an investigation into his allegations, but the NHS found them unproven. The Trust was driven by the need to meet Government-imposed waiting-list targets of 18 weeks for non-urgent surgery, and four hours for emergency admissions. Walker refused to comply and was dismissed from his £150,000-a-year post in 2010. He disputed the charge, claimed unfair dismissal, and was given a £500,000 pay-off in 2011 as part of a compromise agreement, which included a clause requiring him to keep quiet about the circumstances of his sacking.

The controversy surrounding patient safety and the unusually high death rates of patients in the Mid Staffordshire Trust led to a major inquiry (the Francis Report in 2010) published in February 2013. The Lincolnshire Health Trust had also become subject to investigation as one of 14 Trusts with high patient death rates. Walker decided to break his silence by speaking on the BBC Today program on 14 February 2013 about the scandal and its relation to his own dismissal.

NHS lawyers had tried to prevent him from speaking. They wrote: 'Should this interview proceed you will be in clear breach of the agreement and as a result the Trust would be entitled to recover from you the payments made under the agreement and any costs including its legal costs.' After he went ahead with the interview, he received a further letter from lawyers which read: 'The Trust confirms that the Compromise Agreement was never intended to prevent you from raising matters of public interest about patient safety concerns.'

The second letter reflects the true position: ever since the *Public Interest Disclosure Act* 1998, such confidentiality clauses in agreements have been void in so far as they relate to public interest whistleblowing.

Following this incident, the Health Minister wrote to Health Trusts to prevent them using such clauses in the future. He called for the NHS to 'recognise and celebrate' staff who had 'the courage and professional integrity to raise concerns over care'.

The issue is that confidentiality or gagging clauses frequently form part of compromise agreements when staff leave after disputes. Essentially, they provide that neither side will criticize the other. However, UK law seeks to prevent employers from buying whistleblowers' silence. Section 43J of the *Employment Rights Act* states:

1. Any provision in an agreement to which this section applies is void in so far as it purports to preclude the worker from making a protected disclosure.

2. This section applies to any agreement between a worker and his employer (whether a worker's contract or not), including an agreement to refrain from instituting or continuing any proceedings under this Act or any proceedings for breach of contract.

This provision is evidently not well known: compromise agreements are signed by whistleblowers in exchange for pay-offs, and they may feel themselves bound by the agreements even though they are legally void where public interest disclosures are concerned.

Source: Paul Stephenson.

Chapter 9

The United Kingdom

Britain passed the *Public Interest Disclosures Act* (PIDA) in 1998. Two private members bills had attempted to introduce whistleblower protection legislation in 1995 and 1996 but had failed. The third attempt, also a private members bill, was successful. It came into force on 2 July 1999 as an amendment to the *Employment Rights Act* of 1996. It was introduced with the assistance and drafting support of Public Concern at Work (PCaW), the non-government organisation supporting whistleblowers. The early arguments for a whistleblower protection bill revolved around accidents such as that of the sinking of the cross channel ferry, the 'Herald of Free Enterprise', in which 193 people died. The subsequent inquiry found that, on five separate occasions, staff had warned that its bow doors were not closing, but that these warnings were lost at the middle management levels.

PIDA 1998 is significantly different to any US legislation and, as shall be seen, with the Australian systems. PIDA compensates employees who make disclosures of wrongdoing and who suffer retribution as a result. In cases where retribution (such as dismissal or being passed over for advancement) takes place, the employee may bring a case before an Employment Tribunal, which can award compensation.

PIDA 1998 has gone through a number of minor revisions, the more outstanding of which are that: (i) whistleblowers must show a reasonable belief that the disclosure was in the public interest, (i.e. disclosures of a personal employment nature will not be entertained), (ii) the disclosure must be in good faith, (iii) detriment by co-workers can result in a claim against the employer, and (iv) the definition of worker was expanded to include certain types of contractors.

Developments since 1998

By 2009, in a survey undertaken by PCaW of the first ten years of PIDA, some 23 percent of those surveyed indicated that they knew legal protection existed for whistleblowers. Nearly 90 percent said they would raise concerns about possible corruption, and 38 percent said their employer had a whistleblowing program. About 28 percent, however, did not know how and to whom they could raise concerns. Applications to employment tribunals increased markedly, from 157 in 1999/2000 to 1,761 in 2008/09.[1]

Subsequent PCaW studies found that about 81 percent of respondents supported whistleblowing; that 60 percent had raised concerns, but of those, 74 percent were ignored.[2]

The achievements were sufficient for The Whistleblowing Commission, in a PCaW sponsored inquiry into PIDA in 2013, to describe PIDA as having 'rightly been described by the Council of Europe as one of the most comprehensive laws of its kind'.[3] Nevertheless, sufficient concern with the efficacy of the PIDA process was evidenced for PCaW to establish the Commission, and for the government to establish its own inquiry. PCaW's Whistleblowing Commission found a number of improvements were possible for the British system.

The Whistleblowing Commission

One weakness of the British system is that the whistleblower has to first suffer the retaliation. The Commission noted that 'PIDA, albeit indispensable, only provides a remedy when a worker's rights have already been detrimentally affected'.[4] The Commission provided no recommendations on whether this concern should be addressed. Discussions within PCaW and with other whistleblower supporters assert that the possibility that an employer may have to pay damages to a whistleblower will discourage retribution. It is an assertion that is yet to be proven, and, as suggested by the preliminary research outlined below, is of doubtful validity.

Other recommendations of the Commission include an extension of the list of wrongs which ensure whistleblower protection. The six wrongdoings currently listed in the Act are: (i) a criminal offence; (ii) failing to comply with any legal obligation; (iii) a miscarriage of justice; (iv) when the health or safety of any individual is endangered; (v) when the environment is likely to be damaged; and finally, (vi) concealing any of the above matters. The recommended extensions are (vii) a gross waste or mismanagement of funds, and (viii) serious use or abuse of authority. The Commission described this list as 'non-exhaustive.'

The definition of 'public interest' was noted as creating definitional problems. The Commission recommended that the coming government inquiry provide examples, but did not itself attempt to clarify the issue further. It should be noted that the list of (now) eight wrongdoings are possible actions against the public interest by all sectors of the economy – by government agencies, private business and the not-for-profit sector. As such, they do not clarify some wrongs – using government department's resources and equipment without permission, for instance, might readily be considered as against the public interest. Using a company's resources, such as using its computers for private use, may possibly be contrary to the organisation's code of conduct, but it is uncertain whether such actions are contrary to the public interest. Chapter 3 has argued that they are, on the basis that all wrongdoing is against the public interest. A wider agreement on the definition of public interest, however, would be beneficial.

Other recommendations included the following:

- Categories of workers that are covered have been expanded with close to a dozen new categories added, including overseas workers with British companies.

- The gagging clause requirement should be redrafted to make it clearer. Currently the Act precludes gagging clauses that prevent the worker making a protected disclosure. The Commission notes, however, that gagging clauses are 'widely used in all sectors' (p.22). This problem will not be resolved until steps are taken to ensure a whistleblower's complaint goes through to a regulator and is investigated and acted upon.

- The Government institute a recommended Code of Practice. The recommended Code is mainly aimed at establishing internal whistle-blowing procedures, although it does list the conditions when a whistleblower can go to a regulator, or outside to the media or those organisations that the whistleblower believes can action the complaint. The conditions for disclosing to the media are: (i) that the whistleblower does not make the disclosure for personal gain; (ii) it is reasonable to make the disclosure; and (iii) the disclosure is of an exceptionally serious nature.

Priority improvements in the UK system

The most serious UK whistleblowing problem is that documented in an article by Cathy James, Director of PCaW, and outlined in the chapter on regulatory failure.[5] That is, whether or not the wrongdoing is being stopped. The complaint of the whistleblower who has experienced discrimination is heard by the Employment Tribunal. The whistleblower is awarded job restitution and/or such damages as the tribunal feels is appropriate. But a large percentage of submissions are settled out of the Tribunal in a confidential agreement. James claims that overall this means that an outsider, including PCaW, can see information about the whistleblower's concern in only a small percentage of all PIDA claims. The impact of this ability of the employer to buy off the whistleblower was illustrated in Box 8: The National Health Service.

The Commission addressed the problem of employers being able to shut down an enquiry by specifying a reporting system that regulators should adopt (outlined in Chapter 7). A much quicker way to establish whether regulators are stopping wrongdoing is, of course, an immediate one-off study on what a representative sample of regulators are currently doing with the information that they receive. Such a study would ascertain whether or not regulators are stopping the wrongdoing much earlier than would be obtained using a reporting mechanism. If it is found that wrongdoing is not being stopped, then Britain has to move to a system which strengthens direct investigations by the regulators.

The UK system also opens up the possibility of rorting by employees bringing up fictitious whistleblowing cases. An employee can accuse a superior officer in an employing organisation of, for example, bullying. Earlier chapters have given examples of people with personality disorders who may seriously believe the accusation to be true. Other 'whistleblowers' may be more skilled. He or she may even go to the local newspaper or radio station. The organisation has little choice but to reprimand, or even dismiss, the accuser. Hopefully, the Employment Tribunal will see through the accusation and dismiss the case. The Tribunal's task, however, is not to establish the validity of the whistleblower's accusations, but to determine whether he or she has been treated detrimentally, and to award compensation. The Tribunal will determine that the detriment was actual, but it may not determine whether the claim for wrongdoing was factual.

A second problem requiring a decision is whether waiting for the whistleblower to experience the reprisal is in the best interests of building an effective whistleblowing system. In effect, such a system does prohibit the reprisal, as do the US and Australian systems, but it does not have criminal penalties and possible imprisonment attached. On the surface, the latter penalties would appear to be a greater deterrent to taking detrimental action against a whistleblower.

A third issue in the UK is the establishment of an incentive or compensation system for whistleblowers along the lines of the *False Claims Act* and related legislation in the US, as outlined in Chapter 6. As that chapter states, it is difficult to deny the moral validity of that legislation, in that it prevents wrongdoing more effectively than alternative processes, while at the same time freeing up millions of dollars, otherwise stolen, for expenditures on health, education and social welfare programs.

---

[1] Lewis, D 2010, 'Ten years of Public Interest Disclosure Act, 1998 claims. What can we learn from the statistics and recent research?' *Industrial Law Journal*, vol. 3, no. 3, p. 327. The article quotes, inter alia, a PCaW study: Public Concern at Work 2010, *Where's whistleblowing now? Ten years of legal protection for whistleblowers*. PCAW, viewed 1 December 2013, www.pcaw.org.uk/files/PIDA_10year_Final_PDF.pdf.

[2] Public Concern at Work & University of Greenwich 2013, Whistleblowing: The inside story, PCAW, May, viewed 19 June 2013, www.pcaw.org.uk.

[3] The Whistleblowing Commission 2013, Report on the effectiveness of existing arrangements for workplace whistleblowing in the UK, PCaW, November, viewed 29 December 2013, www.pcaw.org.uk/files/WBC percent20Report percent20Final.pdf.

[4] *Ibid.*

[5]James, C 2011, 'Whistleblowing, risk and regulation', in D Lewis & W Vandekerckhove (eds.), *Whistleblowing and democratic values,* Proceedings of the International whistleblowing research network 2011, Middlesex University, London, 23-24 June 2011, *viewed 2 November 2013,* p.115, http://academia.edu/1348441/Whistleblowing_and_Democratic_Values_free_ebook.

Box 9: Weapons of Mass Destruction

Andrew Wilkie

In March 2003, Andrew Wilkie resigned from his position as an analyst with the Australian Office of National Assessments (ONA) and went public in protest over the coming war in Iraq. The ONA assesses and analyses international political, strategic and economic developments for the Prime Minister and senior ministers in the National Security Committee of Cabinet.[1] Wilkie's issue was over the existence of weapons of mass destruction (WMD) in Iraq.

As Wilkie says on his website, he 'was the only serving intelligence official from the Coalition of the Willing to break ranks and publicly resign in the lead up to the war in Iraq.'[2]

Wilkie had resigned over the WMD threat and links to al-Qaeda presented publicly by the then Australian government (the Howard government), in contrast to the more measured assessments of the professional intelligence community. Wilkie came under sustained personal and professional attack from Howard and his media supporters. The Prime Minister later apologised to Wilkie after acknowledging that a member of his staff had leaked untrue allegations to the media about the state of Wilkie's marriage and mental stability.[3]

The words of Senator Johnston, made under Parliamentary privilege, are a measure of the rancour directed against Wilkie.[4]

> *... this very dishonourable affair of a senior, allegedly ABC classified intelligence officer jumping ship and seeking to make a media career out of his former employment as a public servant. How dishonourable and reprehensible ...*

Wilkie moved into a political career, standing against the Prime Minister in Howard's electorate of Bennelong in 2004, but was unsuccessful.[5] He later ran successfully in the 2010 election as an independent in Denison, a Federal seat in Tasmania.

Wilkie's issues, as a federal politician, have been gambling reform, particularly poker machines, the withdrawal of Australian troops from Afghanistan, and whistleblowing reform. Australia had no national whistleblower legislation at the time of his election. He proposed his own Public Interest Disclosure (Whistleblower Protection) Bill 2012, but it was unsuccessful. He supported the subsequent Public Interest Disclosures Act put up by the government, although criticising it for a number of weaknesses, including: (i) no provision for political staffers; (ii) no provision for members of the intelligence community; (iii) the exemptions it provided ministers; and (iv) the restrictions on disclosures to the media.

Wilkie, as reported by the journalist, went further:

> *A strong whistleblower law would present public service mandarins with a dreadful choice: if they fail to address internal complaints about shoddy administration, there would be a strong likelihood that such problems would be featured on the front page of the nation's newspapers. Worse, they would be prevented from seeking revenge on those who reveal their ineptitude to the media.*[6]

Wilkie has also criticised WikiLeaks over the release Iraq war logs, arguing that, while WikiLeaks had an important role to play in outing official misconduct, it should not be reckless and put people at risk.[7]

In 2010, he published his account of the original whistleblowing events in Axis of Deceit: The Extraordinary Story of an Australian Whistleblower.[8]

---

[1] From the ONA website: Office of National Assessments 2013, ONA, Canberra, viewed 22 November 2013, www.ona.gov.au.

[2] From Andrew Wilkie's web site: *Whistleblower protection,* viewed 22 November 2013, www.andrewwilkie.org/content/index.php/awmp/issues_extended/whistleblower_protection.

[3] Kingston, M 2004, *'Andrew Bolt: I did 'go through' leaked top secret report by Wilkie',* Sydney Morning Herald, April 30, viewed 22 November, www.smh.com.au>.

[4] Commonwealth of Australia 2003, Parliamentary debates: Senate: official Hansard, vol. 40, pp. 14836.

[5] John Howard was unseated in the election of 2007 by Maxine McHugh, a journalist. She was only the second person to unseat a sitting Australian prime minister. Howard had been the member for 33 years.

[6] Merritt C 2013, 'Whistleblower bill comes up short', *The Australian*, 22 March, p. 30.

[7] Moses, A 2010, 'Wilkie criticises WikiLeaks over Iraq war dump', Sydney Morning Herald, October 26, viewed 22 November, www.smh.com.au.

[8] Wilkie, A 2010, *Axis of deceit: The extraordinary story of an Australian whistleblower*, Penguin Books, Australia.

Chapter 10

Australia

Australia has weak whistleblower protection laws. As Richard Ackland, a widely-acknowledged legal commentator, stated recently:

> Strong whistleblower laws and defamation laws that recognise responsible journalism are important governance and integrity issues – and we have neither of them.[1]

He noted on the passing of the country's first national whistleblower protection law in 2013:

> What has finally been produced, after a four-year delay, is a damp squib. Members of Parliament and their retinues of staff are exempt and there are "designated publication restrictions" that put whole swathes of territory out of bounds. To avoid civil or criminal liability, the whistleblower must play a game of Twister. [2]

This chapter outlines the whistleblowing legislation and associated administrative practices in Australia. There are three major categories: (i) the recent national law; (ii) the various state whistleblower Acts; and (iii) the whistleblower protections available to the private sector. It also outlines why Ackland and other commentators decry the new national law, and generally why Australian practices cannot be ranked very favourably.

National legislation

The national legislation, the *Public Interest Disclosure Act* 2013, enacted into law in early 2014, contains the same principal legislative obligations encompassed by most legislation in the states and territories of the country.

The new Act replaces the *Public Service Act* 1999, Section 16, 'Protection for whistleblowers'. This original Act is near useless, providing none of the principles for whistleblower protections set out elsewhere in this book.

The new national Act applies to all employees of the Commonwealth of Australia. Its principle features are:[3]

- The person can disclose the information to the Commonwealth Ombudsman, the Inspector General of Intelligence and Security (IGIS), or a prescribed investigative agency.

- Disclosers do not have to identify themselves and may remain anonymous.

- A person need not expressly identify their report of wrongdoing as a public interest disclosure.

- Making a disclosure does not necessarily protect the discloser from the consequences of their own wrongdoing, including where they have been involved in the misconduct they are reporting.

- Agency procedures should protect the discloser's identity. It is a criminal offence for a public official involved in handling a disclosure to reveal the discloser's identifying information to anyone without the discloser's consent.

- The authorised officer must also inform the Ombudsman or the IGIS of the matter. This obligation reflects the oversight role of the Ombudsman and the IGIS.

- Notice of a decision not to investigate must be given to the discloser, provided they are readily contactable.

The following paragraphs set out the principal objections and weaknesses of the legislation as seen by other observers (in addition to Ackland's 'damp squib').

AJ Brown, Professor of Public Policy and Law and Program Leader, Public Integrity and Anti-Corruption in the Centre for Governance and Public Policy, at Griffith University, writes:[4]

> There are still gaps in the scheme – especially lack of protection when public officials report wrongdoing by politicians, and significant exclusions for intelligence agencies. These gaps must be filled in time, along with the yawning gap that remains for whistleblower protection in the private sector.

Suelette Dreyfus, Research Fellow in the Department of Computing and Information Systems at the University of Melbourne, and a specialist in online whistleblowing, asserts that:[5]

- the new act has exclusions for intelligence agencies and the use of intelligence information that result in whistleblowers not being protected in a range of circumstances.

- the bill won't protect people from making disclosures about the conduct of ministers (including the Prime Minister), the Speaker of the House of Representatives, and the President of the Senate in many circumstances.

- media access is still restricted.

According to a 2012 Newspoll, 87 percent of Australians support whistleblowers being able to turn to the media, even if it means revealing inside information in doing so.[6]

Perhaps the weakest aspect of the new legislation is the exclusion of reporting the wrongdoings of ministers from the legislation. As seen in the following paragraphs on the problems with public sector whistleblowing, and in Exhibit 10.2, ministerial wrongdoing is not unknown in Australia.

State whistleblower legislation

Australia has six states and two internal territories. The territories are now self-governing, although their legislation can be overridden at the federal level. Each has whistleblower protection laws and an attendant administrative structure.

Table 10.1, taken from a work by Prof AJ Brown,[7] shows the current legislation in each jurisdiction.

Table 10.1 Current legislation by jurisdiction

No.	Jurisdiction	Current Act	Original Act
1	Commonwealth (Federal)	*Public Interest Disclosure Act* 2013	*Public Service Act* 1999 (s. 16) (continuing)
2	Victoria	*Protected Disclosures Act* 2012	*Whistleblowers Protection Act* 2001[replaced]
3	Australian Capital Territory	*Public Interest Disclosure Act* 2012	*Public Interest Disclosure Act* 1994 [replaced]
4	Western Australia (State)	*Public Interest Disclosure Act* 2003 [amended 2012]	*Public Interest Disclosure Act* 2003
5	New South Wales (State)	*Public Interest Disclosures Act* 1994 [reformed 2010, 2012]	*Protected Disclosures Act* 1994
6	Queensland (State)	*Public Interest Disclosure Act* 2010	*Whistleblowers Protection Act* 1994 [replaced]
7	Northern Territory	*Public Interest Disclosure Act* 2008	*Public Interest Disclosure Act* 2008
8	Tasmania (State)	*Public Interest Disclosures Act* 2002 [amended 2009]	*Public Interest Disclosures Act* 2002
9	South Australia (State)	*Whistleblowers Protection Act* 1993	*Whistleblowers Protection Act* 1993

The coverage of each whistleblower law and the institutions that administer it vary from state to state. All, with the exception of South Australia, have been updated since they were first enacted. The quality and coverage of the legislation, and the types of administering institutions, also vary. Only two states, for instance, provide protection if the disclosure is to the media. Even then, the protection is conditional. The main features of the legislation in each state are summarised in the nine points set out in Exhibit 10.1.

Exhibit 10.1

Protections available under state legislation in Australia

1. Confidentiality for whistleblower's identity is maintained in all states and territories, although with conditions.

2. Reprisals are prohibited in all states & territories.

3. Injunctions against reprisals under the Act can be taken out in all states & territories except South Australia.

4. Proceedings for damages for reprisals can be instigated in all states and territories.

5. The right to relocate is provided in Queensland, the Australian Capital Territory (conditional), Western Australia, and the Northern Territory. Other states do not require the government to offer relocation of the whistleblower as an automatic option.

6. Indemnity against civil and criminal proceedings is provided by all states.

7. Absolute privilege against defamation is offered in all states & territories except South Australia, Western Australia, and Tasmania.

8. Anonymous disclosures allowed in all states & territories except South Australia.

9. Protection, if the wrongdoing is released to the media, is provided in Queensland and NSW, but it is conditional.

Problems of public sector whistleblowers

Whistleblowers in government face a particularly acute set of problems. Public servants work in specialised functions, frequently in issuing permits and licenses to approve or reject the use of land, infrastructure or other resources. The nature of the complaint will often identify the whistleblower, and expose him/her to the possibility of retaliation.

A particular set of issues experienced in one of the Australian states, New South Wales (NSW), further illustrates the difficulty.

The state of NSW changed government after an election in 2011, due, according to widespread media reports, to public disapproval of the considerable graft and corruption under the previous administration. Several ministers in the previous government were subject to inquiries by the Independent Commission Against

Corruption (ICAC). One minister is already in gaol, some have been recommended for judicial prosecution by ICAC, and others are slated for further inquiry. A strong, if not the overriding, reason for this was their use of their ministerial position for personal gain.[8]

And yet not one civil servant blew the whistle on ministerial wrongdoing.

Those familiar with the NSW administration at the time would understand this reluctance. A 2012 study by the NSW Public Service Commission of 130 state agencies and 60,000 employees shows that 30% witnessed improper conduct.[9] Twenty-three percent of those witnesses submitted a formal complaint. None were against ministers subsequently investigated by ICAC. The reason for this reluctance is that civil servants can too easily be targeted for retaliation by their ministers and compliant Heads of Departments.

A whistleblowing incident with which this author is familiar will illustrate the issue further. Exhibit 10.2 provides an actual, although disguised, example. Most public servants will keep quiet. They will likely be so advised, even by people with knowledge of the protective systems available to them.

Exhibit 10.2

A whistleblower's quandary

A colleague related this story. It concerns the question asked of him by a public servant on whether or not to expose a wrongdoing, i.e. to blow the whistle. The three of us got together to help Mark, as we shall call him, to make the decision.

Describing the actual work of many in the public service makes it near-impossible to keep hidden the identity of that person, so this story also has to disguise Mark's actual job.

Mark approved certain types of development applications. In the case in question, he had received an application from a local organisation, and had rejected it. His reasons were that the application violated widely-accepted community values. On the form that he sent up for his Head of Department's signature, the rejection was noted.

Sometime later, he discovered that his Head of Department had changed the application to approved, and had signed the approval. He was extremely surprised, as an approval overrode many years of accepted practice, as well as widely-held community values.

Mark's first question was: 'Why?' The only reason he could think of was that an approval would benefit the local organisation financially. Mark was also fairly sure that this organisation was a financial and political supporter of the Minister. The Minister wanted the application to go ahead and had asked the Head of Department (HoD) to approve it. Mark's HoD had duly complied with the Minister's request. With all heads of departments on renewable contracts, there would be very few that would cross their minister.

Mark first wanted to go public. If it came out into the open, public opinion would force the Minister to recant. But if he leaked to the newspapers, his identity would become known. Mark was well aware that to release information without departmental approval was against the law. He was not going to risk even an anonymous leak.

Other options were available to Mark. One was to approach the HoD directly. Mark rejected this option, however, as he believed it would bring on a confrontation with his HoD. If Mark brought it up as a quiet, non-confrontational question, his HoD could use his authority to assert that approval was the best option in this case. The HoD could also say that it was a ministerial decision, and that the Department was obliged to act as their elected representative requested. Mark could not become too insistent, as it would be unlikely to succeed, and would likely damage his career options and prospects.

Yet another option would be to report to the whistleblowing Ombudsman. Mark could ask for confidentiality, but he could not see the Ombudsman taking any action without it becoming open knowledge where the information came from. In any case, we had also read the local whistleblowing legislation. We were reasonably, but not totally, sure that overriding a public servant's decision was a wrong that qualified for whistleblower protection.

My colleague and I advised his friend to live with it. The Minister would get away with this one.

Hopefully, with the new legislative requirements enacted in 2011 advising public agencies to install 'internal reporting' systems and to appoint public interest disclosure officers, the willingness to speak out will improve. Such disclosure officers will require a particularly strong immunity, however, from ministerial and senior public service pressure.[10]

Corporate whistleblowing

The corporate sector is covered by the whistleblowing provisions of the *Corporations Act* 2001. Given that the public sector makes up only 16% of the workforce, it is reasonable to assume that the bulk of wrongdoing may arise in the private sector.

The whistleblowing provisions in this legislation were introduced in 2004. The body responsible for handling protected disclosures is the Australian Securities and Investments Commission (ASIC).

The Government instituted an inquiry into the efficacy of the whistleblower provisions of the Act in 2009. The government itself stated at the outset of that inquiry that the provisions 'appear to have been poorly regarded and rarely used'. At the time the inquiry was initiated, 'only four whistleblowers had used these protections to provide information to ASIC'.[11]

Twenty-two submissions were received by this inquiry, with 20 cleared for public release. Each submission responded to nine questions posed by the Treasury on optional ways to strengthen whistleblower protection. It should be noted that the majority of responses to the Treasury survey supported major whistleblowing policies put forward in other countries in both public and private sectors. Most respondents advocated strengthening and extending the protections.[12]

The dominant reason for the failure of the Act was that the protections were limited to contraventions of the Act. The incomprehensibility of the *Corporations Act* would also ensure that its whistleblower provisions were nearly useless: "Unlovely and Unloved" is a description of the Act provided by the Associate Professor of Law at Melbourne University.[13] Wrongdoings not covered under this legislation include "health and safety matters, breaches of anti-discrimination laws, environmental damage, waste and corruption".[14]

Details of the *Corporations Act*

Protection under the Act entails that:

> *Persons making such disclosures cannot be subjected to civil and criminal liability, termination of employment, reduction in employment conditions, the enforcement of contractual remedies and/or liability for defamation as a result of the disclosure.*[15]

On the negative side, in addition to the extremely limited coverage, the Act specifies that an anonymous complaint cannot be made. Also, if the individual does not go through the channels designated in the legislation (e.g. he/she goes to the media instead), then there is no protection.[16]

The respondents raised four issues additional to the government's options. They were:

- Managing vexatious 'whistleblowers' was an issue that needed to be sorted out.
- Wrongdoings that should be protected need to be expanded and clarified.
- ASIC (the Australian Securities and Investment Commission) appeared to be an inappropriate agency, from the point of view of relevant competence in resolving issues of corporate malfeasance.
- A full set of protections is required for whistleblowers, including the provision of support in making the exposures.

The above recommendations were made to the Government in 2009. At the date of writing, early 2014, not one had been acted upon.[17]

Related activities

Australian Securities Exchange (ASX)

The ASX introduced whistleblowing provisions in 2007. These are not mandatory, but corporations are required to note non-compliance with ASX recommendations in their yearly company statement. The number of companies who have complied with the recommendations are few. As of 2010:

> *Preliminary findings of an empirical pilot study into the uptake of whistle blowing programs of ASX 200 indicate only 54 per cent of companies having a full whistleblower program linked to their governance frameworks as of concern.*[18]

Australian Standards

Australia has also issued an Australian standard on whistleblowing Whistleblower Protection Program for Entities (AS 8004-2003).[19] It is one of a four part series on corporate governance (AS 8000 Good governance principles):

- AS 8001 Fraud and corruption control
- AS 8002 Organizational codes of conduct
- AS 8003 Corporate social responsibility
- AS 8004 Whistleblower protection programs for entities

This standard draws on the provisions of the Victorian *Whistleblowers Protection Act* 2001. Essentially, it sets out the requirements of whistleblower protective legislation for the public sector as seen over a decade ago.

Why Australia has such a poor record

Ackland argues that the dislike of the 'dobber' runs deep in some Australian institutions.[20] A dobber is a widely-used pejorative term for anybody who betrays their colleagues to those in authority. This reasoning may be correct, but given the clear need for whistleblower protection in other countries, it is difficult to see why the unwillingness in Australia should be particularly greater than elsewhere.

There are some who argue that the unwillingness of Australian legislatures to devise effective whistleblowing systems is a throwback to the early days of its settlement. Settled by convicts, the colony was supervised by the NSW Corps, a specially recruited body that came to be known as the Rum Corps. Several governors lost out in attempting to stop the privileges that the Corps had secured for itself. In 1806, Governor Bligh, of mutiny fame, arrived determined to bring the Corps to heel and to stop their trading in rum. This led to the Rum Rebellion and the deposing of Bligh, but also to the eventual disbanding of the NSW Corps.

The answer probably lies elsewhere. Some speculative answers may lie in comparing the whistleblower support systems in Australia, the US and the UK. The reason why Australia's whistleblowing legislation is close to non-existent is that the whistleblower support bodies in the other countries are noticeably more active than in Australia. Australia's body, Whistleblowers Australia, states on its website that it is 'an association for those who have exposed corruption or any form of malpractice, especially if they were then hindered or abused, and for those who are thinking of exposing it or who wish to support those who are doing so'. It is neither a research body nor an organisation lobbying for strengthening the legislation. The Australian body has also been subject to internal differences of opinions, a major one in Victoria at the turn of the decade, and the second nationally in 2010.

The Australian support can be compared with similar organisations internationally. The United States has at least three organisations: POGO, Project on Government Oversight; GAP, the Government Accountability Project; and the National Whistleblowers Center – all of which have undertaken research on whistleblowing. Each has also contributed to the lessons contained in this book. An example is the *Whistleblower's Handbook*, by Stephen Kohn, Executive Director of the National Whistleblowers Center. The lessons in these chapters have also been drawn from the whistleblowing research from the Ethics Resource Center.

In Britain there is PCaW – Public Concern at Work – which was instrumental in inaugurating the *Public Interest Disclosure Act* 1998. It has a small office of people working full-time with whistleblowers, providing advice and support. In Canada, a country of comparable size to Australia, there is FAIR, the Federal Accountability Initiative for Reform.

Each agency has a website that tries to galvanise their supporters into action, whether it be to lobby Congress, or Parliament. Each has extensive website information and publications that help whistleblowers. FAIR's website states:

> *Our aim is to support legislation and management practices that will provide effective protection for whistleblowers and hence occupational free speech in the workplace.*[21]

The research they undertake is significant. PCaW currently has a top level committee of inquiry examining the effectiveness of the *Public Interest Disclosure Act* 1998.

Whatever the reason, there is little doubt that considerable strengthening of Australia's whistleblowing systems is of high priority.

---

[1] Ackland, R 2013, 'Shield laws leave whistleblowers, reporters on hook', Sydney Morning Herald, April 5, p.33. The new legislation became operational in early 2014.
[2] *Ibid.*
[3] Commonwealth Ombudsman 2013, Agency Guide to the Public Interest Disclosure Act 2013, Commonwealth Ombudsman, Canberra.
[4] Brown, AJ 2013, 'Whistleblowing law now an acid test for federal politicians', The Conversation, web log post, 21 June 2013, viewed 20 Nov 2013, http://theconversation.com/au.
[5] Dreyfus, S 2013, 'Keeping us honest: protecting whistleblowers', The Conversation, web log post, 2 April, viewed 20 May 2013, http://theconversation.com/keeping-us-honest-protecting-whistleblowers-13131.
[6] *Ibid.*

[7] Brown, AJ 2013, 'Towards Ideal whistleblowing legislation? Some lessons from Australia', E *Journal of International and Comparative Labour Studies*, vol. 2, no.3.

[8] Thompson, E 2011, 'The NSW Elections. A tale of hubris, knaves and scallywags', Australian Parliamentary Review, vol. 26, no. 2, p.20.

[9] Ombudsman NSW 2012, *Oversight of the Public interest Disclosures Act* 1994, NSW Ombudsman, Sydney, p.9.

[10] Coultan, M 2013, 'Obeids' rights on water scrutiny', The Australian, October 29.

[11] Bowen, C 2009, Improving Protections for Corporate Whistleblowers: Options Paper, Attorney-General's Department, Canberra, October.

[12] Bowden, P 2010, 'Stopping corporate wrongs' – the effectiveness of Australian whistleblowing reforms' *Australian Journal of Professional and Applied Ethics*, vol.12, pp 55-69.

[13] Jordan, C 2008, 'Unlovely and unloved. Corporate law reform's progeny', Keeping Good Companies – *Journal of Chartered Secretaries Australia*, vol.60, no 3, p.136.

[14] Pascoe, J & Welsh, M 2011, 'Whistleblowing, ethics and corporate culture: theory and practice in Australia', *Common Law World Review*, vol. 40, pp.144-173.

[15] *Ibid.*

[16] Pascoe, J 2010, 'Corporate sector whistleblowing in Australia – Some Empirical Evidence', Keeping Good Companies – *Journal of Chartered Secretaries Australia* , vol.62, no.6, pp. 373-378.

[17] Bowden, *op cit*, (Correct as at date of writing).

[18] Pascoe, *op cit.*

[19] Standards Australia 2003, Whistleblower Protection Programs for Entities, Council of Standards Australia, Sydney, viewed 12 September 2013, http://fraud.govspace.gov.au/files/2010/12/Australian-Standard-8004-2003.pdf.

[20] Ackland, *op cit.*

[21] Protecting whistleblowers who protect the public interest, FAIR, viewed December 1 2013, http://fairwhistleblower.ca.

Box 10: Julian Assange, Bradley Manning, Edward Snowden and John Kiriakou

The following paragraphs provide a brief timeline as well as an update on the current situation for each of these whistleblowers.

Julian Assange

It is in fact doubtful that Julian Assange is a whistleblower. The principle reason why the US is anxious to get hold of him is his publishing of the exposures of Bradley (now Chelsea) Manning. Assange started the Wikileaks website (www.wikileaks.org) in 2006. Early releases included documentation of equipment expenditures and holdings in the war in Afghanistan, and of corruption in Kenya. In 2010, it released the gunship video, supplied to Wikileaks by Manning. Then came the 'Afghan War Diaries'. The same year came the 'Iraq War Logs', followed by the release of over 250,000 confidential US diplomatic cables. Then, in 2011, files on detainees in Guantanamo Bay were also released.

The ethical issues with these releases related to the possibility that Iraqi or Afghanistan citizens who assisted the allied troops may be identified. Early attempts to redact the documents were patchy, although a more thorough screening took place with the later documents.[1]

In November 2010, WikiLeaks began collaborating with major global media organisations to release the documents.

More recently, Assange has fought a Swedish police request, issued in 2010, for questioning in relation to a sexual assault investigation. He has sought refuge in the Ecuadorian Embassy in London since June 2012.

Bradley Manning

In October 2007, at the age of 19, Bradley Manning joined the US Army. Two years later he was sent to Iraq as an intelligence analyst. He contacted Wikileaks in November 2009, and started downloading the Afghan War Diaries and Iraq War Logs. In April 2010, WikiLeaks posted a video of the 2007 Apache helicopter killing of journalists and civilians in Baghdad. It can be watched on YouTube.

Manning contacted a hacker, Adrian Lamo, online, identifying himself as the source of the leaks. Lamo recorded the chats and handed them over to the US Department of Defence and Wired.com, an online news journal. Manning was arrested in Kuwait in May 2010, and charged with leaking classified information.

A series of reports on the Afghan war, based on internal logs, was published by the Guardian, the New York Times and other media groups in mid-2010. Shortly after, the Iraq War Logs were published, detailing civilian deaths, torture, summary executions and war crimes. The embassy cables followed.

Manning was moved to the Quantico military base in the US in July 2010, and held in a solitary cell. On 17 December 2012, Manning turned 25, his third birthday in prison without trial.

His court martial began in June 2013. Cleared of aiding the enemy but found guilty of five espionage charges, he was sentenced to 35 years in prison in August of that year.

The treatment of Manning was unconscionable. A New York Times report states that he was stripped of his clothing at night, remained naked in his cell, and stood naked for inspection in the morning. Such treatment was unjustified 'humiliation' according to his lawyer, David Coombs. A Marine spokesman, Lt Brian Villard, confirmed this treatment, saying it had been imposed by the brig commander, Warrant Officer Denise Barnes, for safety reasons.[2]

Daniel Ellsberg, in Box 3: The Pentagon Papers, is a passionate supporter of Manning and of the program to free Private Manning. Amnesty International is also circulating a petition for the release of Manning.[3]

Edward Snowden

On 6 June 2013, The Guardian journalist Glenn Greenwald reported that the US National Security Agency (NSA) was screening millions of Verizon customers. Verizon is a US-based communications company that started as Bell Atlantic in 1983. That same month the Washington Post and The Guardian alleged that NSA was accessing US internet agencies, including Google and Facebook, under the Prism surveillance program. On 9 June, Edward Snowden spoke out in Hong Kong, explaining that he was the source and why he went public. Snowden then went into hiding. He was described as a traitor by the Speaker of the US House of Representatives, John Boehner. Booz Allen Hamilton, Snowden's employerm fired him for violating its code of ethics.

In July 2013, Edward Snowden applied for temporary asylum in Russia from inside Moscow's airport. Secretary of State John Kerry requested that Russia return the 'fugitive of justice'. Snowden was granted asylum for a year. Robert Menendez, chairman of the US Senate Foreign Relations Committee, described the asylum as a 'setback' for US-Russia relations.

'Edward Snowden is a fugitive who belongs in a United States courtroom, not a free man deserving of asylum in Russia,' he said.[4]

John Kiriakou

Aged 48 at the time of his trial, Kiriakou was a former CIA employee who revealed the torture that was official US policy under the George W Bush administration. He was convicted in October 2012 for violating the

Intelligence Identities Protection Act as he had provided the name of an officer involved in the CIA's Rendition, Detention and Interrogation program to a reporter.

John Kiriakou pleaded guilty and was sentenced to 30 months in a low security prison in Loretto, Pennsylvania.

'In truth, this is my punishment for blowing the whistle on the CIA's illegal torture program and for telling the public that torture was official US government policy,' he wrote in a letter to his lawyer. 'But that's a different story.'[5]

In 2012, Kiriakou received the Joe A Callaway award for Civic Courage by a Community Trust for standing up for constitutional rights. He has written about his activities in *Reluctant Spy: My Secret Life in the CIA's War on Terror*.[6]

---

[1] The exact position of Assange on this issue is unclear. Sources used for this version were: Beckett, C & Ball, J 2012, *Wikileaks: news in the networked era*, Polity, Cambridge.
We steal secrets: the story of wikileaks 2013, motion picture, Jigsaw Productions US. Produced and directed by Alex Gibney. Numerous websites.
[2] Savage, C 2011, 'Soldier in leaks case will be made to sleep naked', The New York Times, March 4, viewed 10 October 2013, www.nytimes.com.
[3] Amnesty International 2013, Support the release of Chelsea Manning, Amnesty International, London, viewed 20 November 2013, <www.amnesty.org/en/appeals-for-action/chelseamanning.
[4] AFP 2013, 'US fury over Edward Snowden's asylum in Russia', The Australian, August 2, viewed 10 October 2013, <http://www.theaustralian.com>.
[5] Lee Ferran May 31, 2013.CIA Whistleblower' John Kiriakou Describes Life in Prison.News,yahoo, com. Viewed, November 5. 2013
[6] 2013 Skyhorse Publishing Company, New York

Chapter 11

Managing the process

The preceding chapters have indicated that improvements are possible in whistleblowing support systems. This chapter brings together those lessons, putting them in the context of an overall process of managing public interest disclosures. The suggestions set out in this chapter are aimed, in part, at the three countries, but also at developing an overall international approach.

Such an examination must start with Transparency International's recommendations in *Guiding principles for whistleblower legislation,*[1] reproduced in Exhibit 11.1. These principles are for whistleblowing legislation, and deserve strong support and endorsement. Those that deserve particular emphasis include:

- The anonymity of the whistleblower and the confidentiality of his/her information be maintained, if so requested. (#13)
- A wide spread of agencies be able to receive the disclosure. (#17, 18)
- National security whistleblowing disclosures are justified, provided no harm is possible to the national interest or to individuals. (#19)

Additionally, a portion of the following guiding princidples are also worthy of attention:

- The savings should go to the whistleblower. (#23)
- At least an annual collection and publication of whistleblowing data should be undertaken. (# 25)[2]

This chapter examines the whistleblowing process from an additional standpoint to that of the legislative framework – that of managing the whistleblowing processes. It has been this writer's long-held belief that effective whistleblowing requires sound administrative practices, along with a workable legislative underpinning. The chapter sets out those administrative practices under three components: the administrative structure, the teaching of whistleblowing, and whistleblowing research. The objective is to facilitate the speaking out against wrongdoing in organisations as a routine public interest activity, open to all.

The administrative structure

High on the list are systems for providing support to whistleblowers. Most employees do not have the fortitude of some of the whistleblowers portrayed in these pages. Many also need practical support in assessing the validity of their complaint, in determining how it could be submitted, and to whom it should be submitted. He or she may often need emotional support as well.

The personal trauma

Blowing the whistle can be a horrendous experience. Even if the whistleblower does not experience retaliation, it can still be very difficult, and is certainly daunting for an ordinary employee. In almost a decade of listening and at times joining in with whistleblowers, this writer has witnessed some of the more unpleasant aspects of human nature when those in the organisation wish to vent their anger on a whistleblower. The retaliation that many whistleblowers have to face suggests that the person blowing the whistle requires extremely strong self-supporting confidence and capabilities.

There are very few studies on the emotional traumas that whistleblowers go through. Toni Hoffman, the Bundaberg nurse whose story was detailed in Box 1, has testified to the strain placed on her. Another study, also of nurses and also in Australia, puts some dimensions on these strains. Australian researchers carried out in-depth interviews with whistleblower nurses, concluding that greater support was needed to tackle the serious emotional consequences of whistleblowing.[3]

Amanda Pollard, one of three 'whistleblowers' to give evidence to the Francis inquiry into the Mid Staffordshire Foundation (see Box 8: The National Health Service), said that she had only decided to publicly criticise the Care Quality Commission, which regulated the NHS, with 'a heavy heart', but felt compelled to do so because of her fears for patient safety, stating: 'Speaking out is not a decision I have taken lightly. It feels like I've barely slept or eaten over the past few weeks.'[4]

Fear and uncertainty in blowing the whistle is further evidenced in accounts of four New Zealand whistleblowers.[5] Three of the stories document the strong concerns of the whistleblowers. In an embezzlement case, the witness was 'very afraid' of speaking out. A rape victim experienced a 'period of concern and doubt about whether she should go public'; a sex abuse victim 'reluctant to identify herself publicly', 'in part because of … what the news media could say'. She also feared retribution 'as a friend of her abuser had visited her house in a menacing manner'.

Then there is the concern with legal action. This writer has seen it in a number of cases with which he has been closely involved. The concern may range from the cost of seeking advice to the worry of being sued. Added to these concerns is the problem of defending oneself if dismissed. An ordinary employee will have little experience with legal confrontation, and little experience, in fact, with the legal community itself. He or she will be unwilling to risk an exposure solely to correct a wrong for which they are not responsible.

If we are to encourage ordinary people to blow the whistle, there are sound arguments for establishing an administrative structure that provides this support. In most countries, two agencies have already been established, one a whistleblower support group, and the second a regulator for that industry or occupation. The following paragraphs offer suggestions on strengthening the activities of those agencies.

Exhibit 11.1

Transparency international
Guiding principles for whistleblower legislation

Transparency International sets out 30 principles, documented below. The first four principles are definitions, discussed in earlier chapters (whistleblowing, protected individuals and disclosures, a broad definition of whistleblowing, and a broad definition of a whistleblower).

The remaining twenty five are:

5. Threshold for whistleblower protection is 'reasonable belief of wrongdoing'.
6. Individuals shall be protected from all forms of retaliation.
7. The identity of the whistleblower may not be disclosed without consent.
8. The burden of proof is on the employer to show that it is not retaliating.
9. Knowingly false disclosures are not protected.
10. Disclosures shall be immune from disciplinary proceedings and liability.
11. Employees may decline to participate in corrupt, illegal or fraudulent acts.
12. Any private rule or agreement is invalid if it obstructs whistleblower protections and rights.
13. Anonymity – full protection shall be granted to anonymous whistleblowers.
14. Whistleblowers whose safety is in jeopardy get personal protection.

15. Whistleblower procedures should be visible and understandable.

16. Individuals may make disclosures to regulatory or oversight agencies.

17. Individuals can disclose to the media, civil society organisations, legal associations, trade unions, or business and/or professional organisations. (Transparency International requires the allegation be of a serious nature, and persistently unaddressed.)

18. A range of accessible disclosure channels should be made available to employees.

19. Disclosure to the media or civil society organisations of national security/official secrets would be justified: in cases of urgent threats to public health, safety or the environment; if an internal disclosure could lead to personal harm or the destruction of evidence; and if the disclosure was not intended or likely to significantly harm national security or individuals.

20. A full range of remedies must cover all direct, indirect and future consequences of any reprisals.

21. Whistleblowers who believe their rights have been violated are entitled to a fair hearing.

22. Whistleblowers shall have the opportunity to provide input into subsequent investigations.

23. Whistleblowers may receive a portion of any funds recovered or fines levied as a result of their disclosure. Other rewards are possible.

24. Stand-alone legislation is preferable to a piecemeal or a sectoral approach.

25. The whistleblower complaints authority should collect and regularly publish (at least annually) data and information regarding the functioning of whistleblower laws.

26. The periodic review of whistleblowing procedures must involve employee organisations, business/employer associations, civil society organisations and academia.

27. Comprehensive training be provided for public sector agencies and corporations.

28. An independent agency shall receive and investigate complaints of retaliation and improper investigations of whistleblower disclosures.

29. Any act of reprisal, or interference with, a whistleblower's disclosure shall be considered misconduct.

30. Valid whistleblower disclosures shall be referred to the appropriate regulatory agencies for follow-up.

Source: Transparency International – Guiding principles for whistleblower legislation, www.transparency.org. Accessed 12 November 2013. The full list should be consulted in a whistleblower inquiry.

A national whistleblower support agency

A whistleblower support group exists in the semi-voluntary agencies or non-government organisations (NGOs) that exist in all countries – Public Concern at Work in the UK, the Government Accountability Project and others in the US, and Whistleblowers Australia in that country.

Most play a valuable role. They help the potential whistleblower assess whether they have a valid case, and provide advice on how and to whom to submit the disclosure. They also help the whistleblower overcome the hesitation and fear of reprisal that all whistleblowers have.

They could play an even more valuable role. They could advise on gathering and assessing the evidence that is necessary. They could then act, in cooperation with the whistleblower, to submit the evidence to the relevant regulator. Some support NGOs already act in this way.

Such an agency could make a major contribution to resolving whistleblower disclosures expeditiously. The voluntary agencies can act in this role, possibly acting under a public endorsement. If there are no voluntary agencies willing to act, then a case can readily be established for creating such a body – e.g. a national whistleblowing ombudsman.[6] The cost would not be great. PCaW operates close to such a service with only eight to ten staff. The whistleblower office in the Securities Exchange Commission in the US has about the same number.

It is also possible for the agency to help resolve the issue that arises in a number of whistleblowing cases – that of whether or not the whistleblower is genuine. The whistleblower may suffer from some personality disorder, or may level an unfounded accusation from dislike toward a supervisor or the employing organisation. A reverse situation occurs when the whistleblower is accused of emotionally unstable disorders. Both concerns are discussed further below.

An interviewer in a whistleblower support role should know from meeting with the whistleblower whether or not there is a genuine and supportable whistleblowing case. If the support agency does not endorse the whistleblower, it is indirectly saying that it does not believe the whistleblower's accusation.

Whistleblowers and personality disorders

On one side of this concern is the allegation made by hostile employers that the whistleblower is emotionally unstable. The issue has surfaced in all countries. Lewis and Vandekerckhove quote a number of references where this has occurred in Britain.[7] The head of the health watchdog the Care Quality Commission, Dame Jo Williams, cast doubt on the mental stability of a high-profile whistleblower, Kay Sheldon, a non-executive director.[8] Similarly, several cases can be quoted in the US of Bradley Manning being portrayed as having personal difficulties.

A convincing picture in Australia is demonstrated by Crikey.com, an online activist blog. Crikey claims that government agencies discredit contentious whistleblowers by using compliant psychologist assessments.[9] Seminars on psychiatric issues were presented to managers of the Australian Taxation Office (ATO) by a psychiatrist.[10] The chairman of the Australian Justice Tribunal stated that, as long as the practice of paying expert witnesses for psychiatric reports on contentious staff remains in force, government agencies like the ATO 'will continue to foster miscarriages of justice that destroy innocent lives'.[11]

The response of a genuine whistleblower, possibly harried by the employing organisation or by its compliant psychologists, is the need to gather evidence that the wrongdoing is factual, as a response to the possible accusation that he/she is 'unstable'.

Another issue in the whistleblowing debate is that of spurious or vexatious whistleblowers. We are all aware of difficult people in the workplace. The many books on this topic are evidence that there is some substance behind the belief that at least some of our fellow workers suffer from personality disorders.[12]

In the inquiry into the need to strengthen the whistleblowing provisions of the *Corporations Act* in Australia, several respondents noted 'that people with a grudge against their company, or against their supervisor, could raise false allegations – such as bullying or displaying favoritism'.[13]

The issue may go beyond spurious whistleblowers to people with deeper emotional problems – corporate psychopaths. There is a growing interest in psychopaths and organisational psychopaths in particular. Clinically, psychopathy is a personality disorder, involving a lack of affective empathy and attachment to others, superficial charisma and charm, manipulation, and the violation of social norms. Perhaps the best known examination of corporate psychopaths is *Snakes in Suits: When Psychopaths Go to Work* by Paul Babiak and Robert D Hare.[14] The extent to which psychopaths are prevalent in the community is difficult to estimate – typical figures are 1 percent of the general population, 25 percent of the prison population and 3.5 percent of the business world.

It is a demanding expectation placed on a volunteer in a whistleblower support agency or an investigative officer in an Ombudsman's office to pick people with personality disorders. Nevertheless, a careful questioning of the circumstances of an alleged wrongdoing would enable most voluntary or Ombudsman staff to decide whether they would support a whistleblower's disclosure to a regulator.

The teaching of whistleblowing

This book has a principal objective of assisting teachers of ethics to bridge the gap between the pure theory of their texts in moral philosophy and the practicalities of whistleblowing in the workplace. Universities and colleges worldwide often stipulate that their students be exposed to ethical thinking in some form. Such a requirement may result in ethics courses being presented in many, sometimes most, departments and faculties. This demand places a difficult task on those who will teach the ethics course. They will, almost invariably, be members of the teaching staff of the faculty or department. Knowledge of the discipline and its ethical difficulties (or a willingness to undertake the research necessary to acquire this knowledge) is the principal requirement for such teaching. A discipline-based teacher may have little or no knowledge of moral or ethical theory, or of whistleblowing practices. This book is intended to provide much of the whistleblowing knowledge. It is particularly aimed at teachers of ethics in philosophy departments. More ethics courses are taught in these departments than in any other department in educational institutions.

Most university or technical college study is a preparation for work. These pages are, therefore, primarily aimed at people who teach ethics to those about to enter the workforce. It is also aimed at those in or who aspire to work in an ethical slot in a company or government agency – e.g. as an ethics officer, as a member of an ethics committee, or in one of the many independent whistleblowing support agencies currently in existence. How much whistleblowing is taught will be dictated by time constraints, staff enthusiasm, and an already packed curriculum or training program. But if the arguments in an earlier chapter are sound – that people wish to work and study in an ethical environment are reluctant to blow the whistle for fear of retribution or the belief that nothing would be done – then a minimum teaching requirement on any course would be the whistleblower protection mechanisms available in that country. This component would cover not only the legislation that is available, but also the safe whistleblowing guidelines outlined in earlier pages.

As noted, these pages particularly encourage moral philosophers to teach whistleblowing on their ethics courses. Such teaching has two advantages. One, it will spread support for whistleblowing practices more widely. Two, it will also provide a supply of people with knowledge of whistleblowing for the increasing number of companies and government departments setting up whistleblower hotlines. Moral philosophers appear reluctant, however. Robert Frederick, a philosopher, produced a compendium on business ethics that has a brief section titled 'Investigation and due process'. It lists a number of arguments that the 'accuser' should weigh up when considering pointing out a wrong, including: the accuser will be 'shunned, ostracised, disliked'; the accusation 'will fatally damage business friendships'; it 'can haunt an employee for the remainder of his or her working days'; and it will be 'time lost from other business pursuits'.[15]

Another example of the reluctance of moral philosophers to embrace whistleblowing is a study on ethics by two widely published philosophers, Julian Baggini and Peter Fosl.[16] Their book, *The Ethics Toolkit*, sets out a series of 'tools' that are intended to assist readers to decide on desirable modes of ethical behaviour. That moral philosophy should guide action is a principal thesis behind the book; it makes no mention of whistleblowing systems.

This reluctance militates against the benefits we gain from people who are prepared to blow the whistle on wrongdoing. It is also contrary to the increasing value that society is placing on whistleblowers. The three women whistleblowers – Sherron Watkins of Enron, Coleen Rowley of the FBI, and Cynthia Cooper of WorldCom – were nominated as Persons of the Year on the cover of Time magazine in 2002. That nomination came out the same year as Frederick's book.

Whistleblowing research and development

The opening pages of this book set out the documented evidence that whistleblowing is effective. The intervening pages have set out some of the problems which, if resolved, would make it even more effective. This section documents a number of those issues. It is an attempt to identify those approaches that, with further research, or developmental efforts, have the potential to turn speaking out against wrongdoing into a commonly-accepted and more effective practice.

Possibly the highest on the list is an identification of those wrongdoings that should trigger whistleblower support if they are disclosed. The list varies from nation to nation. A uniform and widely agreed list would be of immense assistance to those countries setting up new legislative systems. If these wrongs became a universal list, they would also become better known throughout the workforce, and more widely applied from country to country.

A second priority is an examination of why the investigative process appears to disregard some disclosures. Chapter 7 points out a number of the possible causes. Wrongdoing disclosures that do not match the legislative guidelines would be one of the causes. Administrative or regulatory weakness, together with misleading or even false accusations, would be among them.

An arguable third priority would be the adoption of a reward and compensation system in Australia and the UK. The benefits of such a reward system, in stopping the wrongdoing and in terms of the financial benefits to the public purse, are so large that it is difficult to understand the reluctance of these countries to adopt this process.

The adoption of just one whistleblower protection law in both the US and Australia is a fourth priority. To achieve this would first require considerable research to ascertain whether one list of wrongs would cover all sectors and all industries. A preliminary examination would suggest that it is possible.

A fifth priority would be the creation of whistleblower support agencies. Earlier chapters have argued that the average citizen needs help in identifying the legislation under which he or she is covered if they expose a wrong, and help in packaging that information in a way that would facilitate its investigation by a regulator. Some of the present whistleblower support bodies already provide this assistance. Providing imprimatur to this process with the regulators, or even establishing a public support agency such as an Ombudsman with the task of whistleblower support, would strengthen and expand the process.

Finally, issues of government security are the subject of the next chapter. This chapter discusses the response to and treatment of a whistleblower who reveals wrongs committed by the security and defence agencies of his or her government, but which have the counter argument that the government's subsequent actions were taken in the national interest.

[1] Transparency International 2013, *International principles for whistleblower legislation*, Transparency International, Berlin, viewed 12 November 2013, www.transparency.org. The full list should be consulted in further whistleblower inquiries.

[2] The International Chamber of Commerce (ICC) also has published Guidelines on Whistleblowing:
ICC Commission on Anti-Corruption n.d., *ICC Guidelines on Whistleblowing,* The International Chamber of Commerce, viewed 30 September 2013, www.iccwbo.org/.

3 Peters, K, Luck L, Hutchinson, M, Wilkes, L, Andrew, S & Jackson, D 2011, The emotional sequelae of whistleblowing: findings from a qualitative study, Journal of Clinical Nursing, vol. 20, pp 2907-2914.

[4] Sawer, P & Donnelly, L 2013, 'Hospital watchdog "would not spot another Stafford"', *The Telegraph,* 13 January, viewed 14 September 2013, www.telegraph.co.uk.

[5] Hollings, J 2013, 'Let the story go: The role of emotion in the decision-making process of the reluctant, vulnerable witness or whistle-blower', *Journal of Business Ethics,* vol. 114, issue 3, p.501.

[6] The case is made more fully in Bowden, P 2013, 'Whistleblowing needs a mother', *E Journal of Comparative Labour Studies,* vol.2, no. 3, September-October 2013, pp.4-26.

[7] Vandekerckhove, W & Lewis, D 2011, 'Whistleblowing and democratic values', in W Vanderckhove & D Lewis (eds), *Proceedings of the International whistleblowing research network 2011,* Middlesex University, London, 23-24 June 2011, viewed 2 November 2013, http://ssrn.com/abstract=1998293. The authors quote Draper (1994) and Mansbach (2009) in claiming that there are cases in which hostile employers have portrayed *whistleblowers* as mentally *unstable.*

[8] Lakhani, N 2012, 'Exclusive: NHS watchdog claimed that whistleblower Kay Sheldon was "mentally ill"', *The Independent,* 15 August, viewed 2 November 2013, www.independent.co.uk.

[9] Seage, C 2013, 'The tax office, 'hired assassins' and how to gag dissent', Crikey blog, web log post, 5 February, viewed 10 November 2013, www.crikey.com.au.

[10] ibid.

[11] ibid.

[12] Examples are:
Faraday-Brash, L 2012, Vulture Cultures, Australian Academic Press, Brisbane.
Cava, R 2004, Dealing with Difficult People, Firefly Books, New York.
Bernstein, A 2001, Emotional Vampires, McGraw Hill, New York.

[13] Bowden, P 2010, 'Stopping Corporate Wrongs' – the effectiveness of Australian whistleblowing reforms', Australian Journal of Professional and Applied Ethics, vol.12, no. 1 & 2. pp. 55-69.

[14] Babiak, P & Hare, R 2006, Snakes in Suits: When Psychopaths Go to Work, Regan Books, Harper Collins, New York.

[15] Frederick, R 2002, *A Companion to Business Ethics,* Blackwell Publishing, Oxford, p.395.

[16] Baggini, J, & Fosl, P 2007, *The Ethics Toolkit,* Blackwell Publishing, Oxford.

Box 11: The Dreyfus Affair

Georges Picquart,[1] Whistleblower

It is not often realised that there was a whistleblower in the Dreyfus Affair – the 1894 conviction of an innocent man, Alfred Dreyfus, a Jew and a Major in the French Army.

The whistleblower was Colonel Georges Picquart, the Head of French Intelligence. His exposure of the anti-Semitism in the French higher command exhibits a full range of whistleblowing issues. He exposed Dreyfus' trial conviction as a sham, and condemned his subsequent imprisonment on the French penal colony of Devil's Island.

Dreyfus was eventually freed 12 years later, primarily as a result of the efforts of Picquart and the Dreyfusards – a group of Dreyfus' supporters. Contributing to Dreyfus' release was the accusation by Emile Zola, *J'accuse!*, a full front page letter to Félix Faure, President of the Republic, published in the Paris daily, L'Aurore, on January 13, 1898.

The case against Dreyfus began in 1894 when the cleaner in the German military attaché's office, who was in the pay of French Intelligence, would bring the contents of the wastebaskets to French Intelligence, who would then piece them together. One such document, *Le Bordereau*, which showed French artillery dispositions, convinced Military Headquarters that there was a spy was among them. They identified Dreyfus, and, despite the differences in handwriting, had him convicted before a closed military court and sent to Devil's Island. The Defence did not see all evidence against Dreyfus, which was presented to the judges in a 'secret dossier'.

Picquart worked in Military Headquarters. In 1895, he was promoted to head the Intelligence Office, the office that had supplied evidence that had helped to convict Dreyfus the previous year.

In March 1896, the cleaner, Mme Bastian, once again brought in a document, the 'petit blue' which incriminated a Major Esterhazy. Picquart initially thought he had a second spy. However, checking Esterhazy's handwriting (which matched that of *Le Bordereau*), his background, his movements (including visits to the German embassy), and the inconclusive evidence presented at the trial, Picquart realised that Dreyfus had been wrongly accused, and that Esterhazy was implicated in both cases. Through a double agent, Picquart also learned that the Germans knew nothing of Dreyfus. His first move was to expose his findings internally, as most whistleblowers still do. He went to his superior, the Deputy Chief of the General Staff, General Gonse, to the Chief of Staff, General de Boisdeffre, and to the Minister for War, Jean-Baptiste Billot. All three ordered him to keep quiet. To Gonse, Picquart is alleged to have replied: 'I will not carry this secret to my grave.'[2] Picquart received the whistleblower retaliation treatment. He was relieved of his post and sent to Tunisia (October 1986).

Picquart openly blew the whistle in June 1987 through his friend, a lawyer, Fernand Labori, who convinced Auguste Scheurer-Kestner, Vice President of the Senate, to take up Dreyfus' cause, including an open letter to Le Temps newspaper, later renamed Le Monde.

Esterhazy was retired from the military, first undergoing an inquiry (late 1897) and then a trial (early 1898). He was acquitted in both. Picquart was arrested and imprisoned for revealing military secrets the same month.

Zola published *J'accuse!*, ending it with 'Such is thus the simple truth, Mr President, and it is appalling, it will remain a stain on your presidency.' He lauded Picquart's role.

General Bilot and the government instigated the arrest of Zola for libel. Zola lost the court case. The archives of the Manchester Guardian record its opinion of the travesty of the court hearings.[3] The same month Picquart, still in prison, was dismissed from the army (February 1898).

The speeches of Scheurer-Kestner, the activities of prominent Dreyfusards – Marcel Proust, Anatole France, Georges Clemenceau, and Dreyfus' brother Mathieu, finally begin to bear fruit. Picquart was released. The Chamber of Deputies voted for a retrial for Alfred Dreyfus. At the retrial, in Rennes, in August 1899, the military court again found Dreyfus guilty, and sentenced him to ten years. France exploded.

The President of France, with the approval of Cabinet, granted Dreyfus a pardon, which he accepted (19 September 1899). An investigation in 1904 by the Criminal Chamber of Cassation Dreyfus' case found favourably for him. In 1906, the Supreme Court of Appeals found him innocent. He rejoined the army as a Major, and took part in the 1914-1918 war, ending it as a Lieutenant Colonel.

Georges Picquart was exonerated in 1906, and reinstated as a Brigadier General, the rank he would have been expected to reach. He was asked by Georges Clemenceau, then Prime Minister of France, to be Minister for War. He accepted.

Georges Picquart died as a result of a riding accident in 1914.

Georges Picquart, according to any definition used today, was a whistleblower. He initially used internal channels, was unsuccessful, suffered on account of his exposure, and was not ultimately successful until he went public. He also went public at a level that would ensure action.

The Dreyfus affair raises even more pertinent issues, still unresolved today.

It pits the truth of an open and just society against the power of the military establishment. The Generals argued against Picquart, asserting the preservation of the nation, the army and national security had a higher claim than redressing a wrong. The level of justice to be expected from a military court is another issue that Western nations are facing today.

---

[1] This retelling draws on many sources, principally Barbara Tuchman, 1966, The Proud Tower, Hamish Hamilton, London, pp 175-226. As well as numerous websites including Chronology of the Dreyfus Affair, May 2000 by Jean-Max Guieu of Georgetown University. Piers Paul Reid 2012, The Dreyfus Affair, Bloomsbury Press, London gives a pro-catholic view. A very readable version, told from Picquart's personal viewpoint, historically accurate, is Robert Harris, 2013, An Officer and a Spy, Hutchinson, London.

[2] Evidence at the Rennes trial of Dreyfus, 1898.

[3] 24 February 1898: M. Zola Victim of Show Trial www.theguardian.com/theguardian/2011/feb/24/archive-zola-trial-dreyfus-affair-1898.

Chapter 12

National security

A whistleblowing issue of more recent origin than the supply of faulty equipment to the Union armies in the US Civil War is the exposing of activities, taken by governments and government agencies, in the national interest that are considered a wrong. Whether the exposure is about activities such as torturing captured combatants, eavesdropping on allies as well as on enemies, or many of the dubious acts of war, such exposures have been highly controversial in recent years. Some have argued that the revealing of these wrongs is in the public interest, and that the whistleblowers should be protected. Others will regard these 'whistleblowers' as akin to traitors and, in some cases, call for the death penalty.

The issues are complex and divisive, with strong beliefs on either side. This chapter attempts to analyse those issues. It bases this analysis on the actions of Julian Assange, Bradley Manning, Edward Snowden and John Kiriakou, and the reactions of their governments, the media, and the general populace. A brief background for each of these players was set out in Box 10. The majority of these issues lie with the US government, but not all. Australia and the UK have experienced some of these issues, as discussed in the following paragraphs.

The examination will be set out under three concerns:

1. When is it OK to expose an ostensible wrong action by a government acting in the name of national security?

2. Whether we, the general public, have the right to know of these and related actions.

3. Whether a balance of good over bad, right over wrong, is established by revealing these actions.

Has a wrongdoing been exposed?

An earlier chapter examined the issue of what is a wrongdoing, and came to the conclusion that the existing moral theories are of little or no help to a whistleblower in establishing what constitutes a wrongdoing. The whistleblower must rely on the lists of wrongs that the various national legislatures have established.

None of those lists provide any assistance in deciding whether the actions exposed by Assange, Manning, Snowden, etc., were wrong. They provide little help in deciding whether the exposing itself was wrong. We know some of the actual actions exposed are wrong – torture, for instance, is banned by an international convention.[1] One could, therefore, surmise that the revelations of John Kiriakou, who exposed the waterboarding of Guantanamo Bay detainees, would be regarded as acceptable. He exposed a wrong that was not covered under any legislation; and yet he was imprisoned.

The shooting or killing of unarmed civilians is, of course, wrong. In times of war, confusion and uncertainty exist, with the result that we have developed the phrase 'collateral damage'. It is a phrase that brings with it the implication that the killing of civilians can be partially justified. The exposures by Bradley Manning of the Apache helicopter gunship attack in Bagdad, when children and civilians, together with Reuters' correspondents, were killed might therefore be passed off as an unfortunate accident. The callousness of the attackers, one saying that the victims should not have brought their children to a war zone, is disconcerting but not immoral. But, as a later section argues, it is nevertheless information that we have a right to know. It will also be argued that we have that right only if no larger wrong is caused by the revelations.

Violations of the code of conduct of a just war are wrongs.[2] The Mai Lai massacre by Lieutenant William Calley over forty years ago is just such an example.[3] Calley was sentenced to life imprisonment, but subsequently placed under house arrest by President Nixon. Abu Ghraib was another such revelation. There was a whistleblower in each case.[4] Joe Darby, the Abu Ghraib whistleblower, suffered considerable retaliation.[5] Promised anonymity, he was subsequently named by Donald Rumsfeld, the then US Secretary of Defence.[6] Generally, however, revealing these wrongs was considered justifiable.

Manning's helicopter gunship exposure was not considered justifiable by the US government. Other revelations of Manning – the Afghan War Diaries and the Iraq War Logs, and the diplomatic papers – did not expose wrongs. But they have equally been criticised. Nevertheless, as shall be argued, they were revealing information that we have a right to know.

The revelations of Edward Snowden that the National Security Agency in the US intercepted internet traffic and phone conversations are less clear. The bugging of potential aggressors cannot be clearly classified as wrongs – they might even be categorised as necessary steps in maintaining national defences. The bugging of friends and allies is much less defensible. In an ideal world at peace, such interception is indefensible. In a world currently on edge with the tensions of terrorist activities, bugging may be defensible.

But, again, it is our right to know. We may suspect that our security agencies are eavesdropping on others. But to be told that it is happening will spark the necessary debate on how much, how far.

The right to know

There are multiple arguments against the actions of Assange, Manning and Snowden. The more cogent are those that say the activities of police, armies and security organisations have to be secret. Political decision-making and diplomatic interchange must also be able to be kept secret. The arguments essentially assert that politicians, or nations, cannot arrive at an agreed position if every step in the negotiations or in the making of that decision is made public.

That argument is extended for Snowden – that he did his country a great disservice by revealing the extent of his country's snooping. He has alienated allies of the United States and Australia by revealing that the phones of outwardly friendly leaders were hacked.

This chapter argues that this is not so; that provided no harm is done to us or anyone else, Snowden and Manning did no wrong. This assertion is based on two factors – our right to know, and the ethical acceptability of their actions. This immediate section assesses the first assertion – that we, as citizens in a democracy, have a right to know what our politicians are saying and doing. This argument is based on the social contract, a long explored concept of the relationship that exists between the governed and the governors.

Social contract theory reflects the beliefs of several influential thinkers over time, Thomas Hobbes, John Locke and Jean-Jacques Rousseau being among them. Some assert that the concept arose as early as Plato, in the Crito, where Aristotle placed himself at the will of the general populace. The theory essentially states that government exists to ensure the maintaining of our natural rights (Locke), or to meet the interests of society (Rousseau's general will). In either case, it can reasonably be asserted that a government is there to do what its people wish. It responds to the needs and desires of those who elect it.

This assertion of the extent to which we should be kept informed is relatively straightforward. We may argue over what are our natural rights, or even what is the general will, but we exist in a democracy where each decides on his or her choice of political leader. If I am to make a choice on this candidate, or this political offer, I need to know not only what he or she or their political party tells me and how they advocate a particular position, but also what they actually have done and will do. If I am uncertain, or do not find out, I am free to search for a more suitable contract. Such an argument does not assert that a politician or a diplomat cannot be secretive. They have that right as much as anyone. But if that information be a human rights violation or if it affects a democratic right to know, then I am entitled to have that information. And anyone who passes on that information is not stealing, for it is our right to know that information.

Justification of the actions of Edward Snowden relies on social contract theory, as much as do the actions of Bradley (now Chelsea) Manning. I may suspect that my government is bugging other countries and their heads of state, but I would prefer to know for certain. I may agree with it in times of war. In times of peace, I may believe that this action is wrong. If I know what my government is doing, and I disagree, I will voice my disagreement.

Right and wrong, for good or bad

The release of any information has to be balanced against any harm that it may do. The ethical issues with Manning's releases related to the possibility that Iraqi or Afghanistan citizens who had assisted allied troops could have been identified. Early attempts by Assange and his co-publishers to redact the documents were patchy, a source of some tension between them. As noted earlier, a more thorough screening took place on later documents.[7]

Bradley Manning, however, undertook only a minimal check of the documents for any damaging consequences. There were too many, and he was only one person. It could be argued, then, that Manning's actions put lives at risk, and that his actions, therefore, were morally unacceptable. Manning made a choice, whether to release the gunship collateral damage video or to continue with its concealment. He chose to release it. As his defence counsel stated at his trial:

> "Perhaps his biggest crime is that he cared about the loss of life," Coombs said of Manning, asking the judge to account for his pure intentions. Manning explained in February that he was disturbed by the "seemingly delightful bloodlust" his fellow soldiers displayed.[8]

The Snowden exposures are simpler to evaluate – although the debate as to whether he acted ethically is still very active. Snowden released information about the eavesdropping by the National Security Agency in the United States of transatlantic telephone and email conversations, as well as the bugging of the mobile phones of US allies including the German Chancellor Angela Merkel. The negative side of the Snowden revelations has been the damage inflicted on the US with key allies. The US has asked that Snowden be released from his refuge in Russia and that he stand trial in the US. The US Attorney General, Eric Holder, has publicly stated that they will not seek the death penalty, and that Snowden would be issued a passport to travel back to the US.[9] Snowden has clearly broken any agreement he made with his employer – Booz, Allen and Hamilton. Many would argue, however, that the greater good – telling people what they need to know in order to be fully informed members of society – outweighs the law.

The phone tapping of the Indonesian president Bambang Susilo Yudhoyono – and that of his wife and eight of his aides by Australian security forces in the Defence Signals Directorate – was also a Snowden release. The release of this information has generated controversy in both countries. Indonesian anger has been manifest, with the President demanding an explanation and an apology, coupled with demonstrations and burning of the Australian flag outside its embassy in Jakarta. The realisation that for Snowden to have this information indicated that it was also available to the United States possibly increased the anger. The refusal of the Australian Prime Minister to apologise may also not have helped Australian Indonesian relations.

The role of the media

The role of the media raises a number of issues, too. The broadcasting of the news contained in the releases has been a necessary component for all whistleblowers to get their messages out. The differences between Assange himself and the media outlets he used – the New York Times, Washington Post, The Guardian, Sydney Morning Herald, etc. – has become unclear. If Assange were to be charged, these newspapers should also be charged. But this action is unlikely, as they would have the defence of free speech. The US may not prosecute Julian Assange for publishing leaked documents for the same reason, according to reports by the Washington post, citing unnamed US officials.[10]

The Snowden information on Australian spying has initiated a media furore in that country. The information was released by The Guardian Australia and the Australian Broadcasting Commission. Both have been fiercely attacked for releasing the Snowden information, primarily by the News Corporation press. The Melbourne-based Herald Sun's Andrew Bolt wrote that: 'The media … have now damaged our relationship with Indonesia by revealing news against the national interest about activities that were in the national interest'.[11]

Other newspapers have joined in. The UK's Daily Mail went so far as to accuse The Guardian of being the 'paper that helps Britain's enemies'. The Guardian itself reported the criticism that the government has levelled against it: 'Foreign secretary William Hague backs claims by MI5 and MI6 that NSA disclosures have endangered UK's national security'.[12]

In a recent response, 30 editors from around the world, including Fairfax Media's editorial director, Garry Linnell, Age editor-in-chef Andrew Holden and Sydney Morning Herald editor-in-chief Darren Goodsir, backed The Guardian for publishing the Snowden documents, with Linnell saying that such criticism 'hints at a profound and alarming complacency about the roles of media and government'.[13] The divide in the media is reflected in the divide in public opinion.

The role of government

There can be little doubt that governments worldwide are opposed to whistleblowing on security issues. GAP, the Government Accountability Project, on its website states that the US government is not willing to relax its position on these issues. It makes the clear statement:

> *There can be no doubt the unprecedented number of whistleblower indictments we are seeing today, enabled by the Espionage Act of 1917 and*

prosecuted under the Obama administration, are intended to have a chilling effect on all whistleblowers, present and future.[14]

In the UK, David Miranda, the partner of Guardian journalist Glenn Greenwald, who originally broke the Snowden revelations, was recently detained for nine hours at London's Heathrow Airport. He was questioned under a UK anti-terrorism law where authorities confiscated his laptop, cell phone and other electronic devices. The Free Press, a pro media blog, also reports that British authorities oversaw the destruction of computers and hard drives at the Guardian's London headquarters.[15]

The extent to which governments can come to grips with the exposing of wrongs by the security agencies is an unresolved issue. There have been tentative steps in this direction. The US President has apologised to the German Chancellor, and instigated steps to restrict the eavesdropping by the National Security Agency. He has also has conceded that Edward Snowden's revelations should provoke 'the debate we have to have' on the question of who guards the guardians.[16]

But a broad overview policy is yet to come. Possibly it lies in a commitment to assessing the potential for measurable harm against maintaining the right of a free press in maintaining the structure of a democratic system. At least one proposal for a whistleblower protection system for members of the intelligence community has been put forward. It was proposed by Andrew Wilkie, a former member of the intelligence community, and also a whistleblower and now a politician (see Box 9: Weapons of Mass Destruction).

More than 500 of the world's leading authors, including five Nobel prize winners, have condemned the scale of state surveillance revealed by Edward Snowden, and warned that spy agencies are undermining democracy and must be curbed by a new international charter.[17]

Their call comes a day after the heads of the world's leading technology companies demanded sweeping changes to surveillance laws to help preserve the public's trust in the internet – reflecting the growing global momentum for a proper review of mass snooping capabilities in countries such as the US and the UK, which have been the pioneers in the field.[18] Microsoft has made a similar statement.[19]

The US and the UK may have been pioneers, but, as noted above, Australia is not exempt. Perhaps reform also lies in the statements of UN Human Rights Chief Navi Pillay, who has called on all countries to protect the rights of those who uncover abuses. In that same statement, she also stressed the need to respect the right for people to seek asylum. Commenting on Edward Snowden, Pillay noted: 'National legal systems must ensure that there are adequate avenues for individuals disclosing violations of human rights to express their concern without fear of reprisals'.[20]

---

[1] The United Nations Convention against Torture and Other Cruel, Inhuman or Degrading Treatment or Punishment was ratified in 1987. It defines torture as "Any act by which severe

pain or suffering, whether physical or mental, is intentionally inflicted on a person for such purposes as obtaining from him or a third person, information or a confession, punishing him for an act he or a third person has committed or is suspected of having committed".

[2] e.g. The 1949 Geneva Convention.

[3] 'My Lai massacre: Lt William Calley apologises more than 40 years after Vietnam' 2009, The Telegraph, 22 August, viewed 25 November 2013, www.telegraph.co.uk.

[4] Vaughn, R 2013, *Successes and Failures of Whistleblower Laws*, Edward Elgar, Cheltenham, UK.

[5] Bryan D 2007, 'Abu Ghraib whistleblower's ordeal', BBC, 5 August, viewed December 5 2013, http://news.bbc.co.uk.

[6] *ibid.*

[7] Beckett, C & Ball, J 2012, Wikileaks: News in the Networked Era, Polity, Cambridge

[8] Fuller, N 2013, 'Govt. calls for 60 years; defense argues for Bradley's life: trial report, day 36', Bradley Manning Support Network, August 19, viewed 12 November 2013, www.privatemanning.org/news/govt-calls-for-60-years-in-jail-defense-asks-judge-to-let-manning-have-a-life-trial-report-day-36.

[9] Schmidt, MS, Myers, SL 2013, 'U.S. Letter Says Leaker Won't Face Death Penalty', New York Times, July 26, viewed 1 November 2013, www.nytimes.com.

[10] AFP 2013, 'US unlikely to prosecute Julian Assange for publishing leaked documents', The Economic Times,
 27 Nov, viewed 27 November 2013, http://economictimes.indiatimes.com.

[11] Alcorn, G 2013, 'Spies, journalists and inconvenient truths', Sydney Morning Herald, November 22.

[12] Sparrow, A 2013, 'Guardian faces fresh criticism over Edward Snowden revelations' ,The Guardian, 11 November 2013, viewed 12 November 2013, www.theguardian.com.

[13] Alcorn, G 2013, op. cit.

[14] Government Accountability Project, 2013, email 14 July, viewed 20 November 2013, http://lists.topica.com/lists/BW-Events/read/message.html?sort=d&mid=1722721024.

[15] 'End the intimidation of Journalists', Free Press blog, web log blog, August 19 2013, viewed 30 November 2013, www.freepress.net/blog/2013/08/19/end-intimidation-journalists-and-their-families-now.

[16] Although a Guardian columnist is not as readily convinced: Hoelzer, J 2013, 'If Obama wanted an 'open debate' on NSA spying, why thwart one for so long?', *The Guardian*, 14 August, viewed 1 December 2013, www.theguardian.com.

[17] Taylor, M & Hopkins, N 2013, 'World's leading authors: state surveillance of personal data is theft', The Guardian, 10 December, viewed 10 December 2013, www.theguardian.com.

[18] Roberts, D & Kiss, J 2013, 'Twitter, facebook and more demand sweeping changes to US surveillance. AOL, Yahoo, Microsoft, Google, Apple and LinkedIn to call for reforms to restore the public's trust in the internet', The Guardian, 10 December, viewed 10 December 2013, www.theguardian.com.

[19] The man who may be Microsoft's next chief executive (Satya Nadella) says governments must restore trust in technology after NSA revelations: Dredge, S 2013, 'The surveillance system has to be reformed' The Guardian, 11 December, viewed 11 Dec. 2013, www.theguardian.com.

[20] 'UN human rights chief says whistleblowers need protection', 2013, RT Question More blog, web log blog, July 13, viewed 1 August 2013, http://rt.com/news/un-chief-snowden-protection-048.

Box 12: A National Security Story

The Whistleblowers of 1777

Stephen Kohn of the National Whistleblowers Center told a whistleblower story on June 12, 2011 in the opinion pages of the New York Times that went back to the American Revolutionary War. It was written in the light of the controversies over Bradley Manning and other national security whistleblowers. Here is what he said:

In the winter of 1777, months after the signing of the Declaration of Independence, the American warship Warren was anchored outside of Providence, R.I. On board, 10 revolutionary sailors and marines met in secret — not to plot against the king's armies, but to discuss their concerns about the commander of the Continental Navy, Commodore Esek Hopkins. They knew the risks: Hopkins came from a powerful family; his brother was a former governor of Rhode Island and a signer of the declaration.

Hopkins had participated in the torture of captured British sailors; he "treated prisoners in the most inhuman and barbarous manner," his subordinates wrote in a petition.

One whistle-blower, a Marine captain named John Grannis, was selected to present the petition to the Continental Congress, which voted on March 26, 1777, to suspend Hopkins from his post.

The case did not end there. Hopkins, infuriated, immediately retaliated. He filed a criminal libel suit in Rhode Island against the whistle-blowers. Two of them who happened to be in Rhode Island — Samuel Shaw, a midshipman, and Richard Marven, a third lieutenant — were jailed. In a petition read to Congress on July 23, 1778, they pleaded that they had been "arrested for doing what they then believed and still believe was nothing but their duty."

Later that month, without any recorded dissent, Congress enacted America's first whistle-blower-protection law: "That it is the duty of all persons in the service of the United States, as well as all other inhabitants thereof, to give the earliest information to Congress or any other proper authority of any misconduct, frauds or misdemeanors committed by any officers or persons in the service of these states, which may come to their knowledge."

Congress did not stop there. It wanted to ensure that the whistle-blowers would have excellent legal counsel to fight against the libel charges, and despite the financial hardships of the new republic, it authorized payment for the legal fees of Marven and Shaw.

Congress did not hide behind government secrecy edicts, even though the nation was at war. Instead, it authorized the full release of all records related to the removal of Hopkins. No "state secret" privilege was invoked. The whistle-blowers did not need to use a Freedom of Information Act to obtain documents to vindicate themselves. There was no attempt to hide the fact that whistle-blowers had accused a Navy commander of mistreating prisoners.

Armed with Congress's support, the whistle-blowers put on a strong defense, and won their case in court. And true to its word, Congress on May 22, 1779, provided $1,418 to cover costs associated with the whistle-blowers' defense. One "Sam Adams" was directed to ensure that their Rhode Island lawyer, William Channing, was paid.

Nearly two centuries later, the Supreme Court justice William O. Douglas, praising the founders' commitment to freedom of speech, wrote: "The dominant purpose of the First Amendment was to prohibit the widespread practice of government suppression of embarrassing information."

A 1989 law was supposed to protect federal employees who expose fraud and misconduct from retaliation. But over the years, these protections have been completely undermined. One loophole gives the government the absolute right to strip employees of their security clearances and fire them, without judicial review. Another bars employees of the National Security Agency and the Central Intelligence Agency from any coverage under the law. And Congress has barred national security whistle-blowers who are fired for exposing wrongdoing from obtaining protection in federal court.

It is no surprise that honest citizens who witness waste, fraud and abuse in national security programs but lack legal protections are silenced or forced to turn to unauthorized methods to expose malfeasance, incompetence or negligence.

Instead of ignoring and intimidating whistle-blowers, Congress and the executive branch would do well to follow the example of the Continental Congress, by supporting and shielding them.

Original source: Stephen M Kohn. Stephen is the executive director of the National Whistleblowers Center and the author of The Whistleblower's Handbook: A Step-by-Step Guide to Doing What's Right and Protecting Yourself. *His source is www.earlsalisbury.com, Colonial History, under 'Congress suspends Hopkins'.*

Index